love always

365 Daily Devotions for Couples

BroadStreet

PUBLISHING

BroadStreet Publishing Group, LLC.
Savage, Minnesota, USA
Broadstreetpublishing.com

love always

© 2023 by BroadStreet Publishing®

9781424565719
9781424565726 (eBook)

Devotional entries composed by Brenna Stockman.

Typesetting and design by Garborg Design Works | garborgdesign.com
Editorial services by Sarah Eral and Michelle Winger | literallyprecise.com

Printed in China.

23 24 25 26 27 28 29 7 6 5 4 3 2 1

"Love each other deeply,
as much as
I have loved you."

John 15:12 TPT

INTRODUCTION

Love. According to 1 Corinthians 13:7, "It always protects, always trusts, always hopes, always perseveres." *Always.* There's a word that we would rather ignore. Is it even possible to always choose love?

The first days or weeks of marriage might feel easy; loving your spouse is as natural as breathing. But if you've been married for longer than a month, you've likely run into times when choosing love requires effort—sometimes a *lot* of effort. What would it look like to always protect each other? How can you trust when trust has been broken? Is there hope for a relationship that feels like a constant struggle? What can you do to persevere in the moments you want to yell, cry, throw things, run away, or do all of the above?

Commit your marriage to God. Spend time in his presence together. Keep short accounts. Say sorry. Forgive quickly. Use this devotional as a tool strengthen your marriage. It will encourage you to dive into God's Word, seek his wisdom, ask for help, and lean into his love. You cannot always choose love in your own strength, but everything is possible with God, and God is love. So, you can love because he loves you—always.

January

Be completely humble and gentle;

be patient, bearing with one another

in love. Make every effort to keep

the unity of the Spirit through

the bond of peace.

Ephesians 4:2-3 niv

POSSIBLE

Looking at them, Jesus said, "With people it is impossible,
but not with God; for all things are possible with God."

MARK 10:27 NASB

How often do we tell God our deepest desires? As children, we have no problem praying for a ballgame win or a new baby brother, but as adults, we tend to lose the art of entrusting our dreams to the Lord. Maybe we keep a mental list of the times he hasn't answered our prayers the way we wanted, or we might think he has better things to do. Either way, we have to reawaken the inner child who longs to open up to the Lord and trust him in all things.

The Bible is clear that prayer is important in our spiritual lives. One, we need to be reminded that God can do anything. Two, we need to exercise our vulnerability and humility. We need to verbally make our petitions known to God and verbally submit to his plan, whatever it is, just like Jesus did in the garden of Gethsemane. God's power is unsearchable. He can, and does, work miracles for his kingdom. Don't be afraid to ask him what you've been afraid to think about. Trust that he will answer you in the best way.

Lord, we praise you for your great power. You created the world with your words; you can do anything. Remind us that we can trust you with our requests in faith. You work everything together for good.

MUNDANE MATTERS

I want you to understand what really matters, so that you may live pure and blameless lives until the day of Christ's return.
PHILIPPIANS 1:10 NLT

Most people struggle with the mundane tasks of everyday life. Do they really matter? What eternal weight do they carry? Wouldn't our precious time and effort be better spent on more important things? As holy as that sounds, God has given us simple tasks because they can teach us about him. For instance, God is patient. He also esteems the lowly, prioritizes servanthood and care of others, honesty, and humility.

Today, if you are doing your taxes, changing dirty diapers, heading to a mediocre job, washing dishes, or caught up in thankless responsibilities, remember how Jesus also paid taxes, washed feet, worked as a carpenter, and lived a regular life pure and blameless. Do not become dismayed. These trite tasks matter too, and your Father sees you.

Oh God, sometimes it's hard to keep blameless and pure in our daily duties! Please encourage us and remind us to encourage each other too. Thank you for the example of your life.

FIRST

We love,
because He first loved us.
1 JOHN 4:19 NKJV

A good relationship is not made of two people who each give fifty percent. A good relationship is made of two people who are willing to give all when their partner gives nothing, to love their partner first before receiving love or even civility. Some days, we have to give our all. Other days, we are in a spiritual rut, and our spouses are the ones going the extra mile while we refuse to or can't lift our feet.

This is the precedent God set; he loved us before we loved him. A love like this is a true marker of commitment. It shows the other person that we are there for them even when they are at their worst, and we won't abandon them. The prophet Hosea was made to demonstrate this to an adulterous wife who, for all we know, never returned the love he poured over her year after year. We have a high standard to live up to.

Gracious Lord in heaven, you have planted in us the seed of love to grow, flourish, and give you glory. Teach us to show love to those who show us none and to be the one who loves first.

MADE NEW

If anyone is in Christ, this person is a new creation;
the old things passed away;
behold, new things have come.

2 CORINTHIANS 5:17 NASB

We need eyes to see situations and people the way God does. We are not defined by our pasts, and we have no right to define someone else by theirs either. Christ forgave even the worst people when they showed a desire to change. Murderers, adulterers, and thieves clamored for him to make them new!

On a smaller, more personal note, we can't hold the past sins of a spouse against them if they are sorry and working to change. Arguments that begin with "You always" or "You never" don't lead to a good place. Dragging up offenses of the past when dealing with the present is not good game play. When dealing with us, God deals with the current us. He doesn't define us by our past offenses. His forgiveness is final. Let's choose to be grateful and learn from his example.

Lord, this is a new year and a new day. Thank you for not holding our past mistakes against us but always leading us onward and upward. Please teach us to have the same forgiveness and patience with each other.

COURAGE AND FAITH

We are not like those who turn away from God to their own destruction. We are the faithful ones, whose souls will be saved.
HEBREWS 10:39 NLT

The Lord wants us to courageously live like Christ in a world that doesn't respect him or his way of doing things. How we speak, act, and make decisions will be confusing to a population rooted in self-interest and temporary living. Even our marriages look different because they exist to serve him rather than ourselves.

It won't always be easy to swim against the current of this culture, but our faith in the Lord provides us the courage and assurance we need to stay strong and continue. Take the path less trodden, read his Word to light your way, and lean on your spouse when times get hard. Marriage provides a wonderful partnership to help us along the way.

Father God, we are your faithful ones. At times we stumble, and we're not always faithful, but our faith is always in you. We know we can rely on you, and that confidence influences every aspect of our lives. Thank you for calling us your children and providing us a way.

Newly Married

"When a man has taken a new wife, he shall not go out to war or be charged with any business; he shall be free at home one year, and bring happiness to his wife whom he has taken."

DEUTERONOMY 24:5 NKJV

Isn't this an incredible mandate God gave the Israelites? Clearly, God takes marriage seriously, and he knows how important a solid foundation is. Although this Old Testament law is not as applicable in modern society, the principle behind it can still be respected.

While enjoying wedded bliss, build those strong foundations before jumping back into normal life. No matter how far along in our marriage journey we are, let's take time to enjoy each other's company and always spend focused time within each other's love and happiness.

Heavenly Father, we are grateful for our marriage that uses you as its foundation and love as its pillars. Please remind us to prioritize our time together and bring happiness to each other.

GOD'S SUPPLY

My God will supply all your needs
according to His riches in glory in Christ Jesus.
PHILIPPIANS 4:19 NASB

Have you ever been at the end of your rope and God miraculously came through for you? When you have a need and you don't know how to fill it, where do you turn to first? Do you worry? Work harder? Pray?

God has riches beyond our wildest imagination. God lacks nothing, and he wants to share everything with us. More than paying a bill or meeting a deadline, however, God cares about your heart and your faith. He wants you to trust him in moments of need as well as moments of plenty. Yes, we ought to work hard and take responsibility for our lives, but the first thing we should do is call out to our loving, caring, generous Father and ask him for his help and supply.

Dear God, we come to you with our needs today before we try to fill them ourselves. Please supply us with everything we require. Above money, food, answers, or relationships, we pray you would give us faith, courage, love, and peace. We know situations will work out for the best when we trust you.

LIVING IN FREEDOM

Are you bound to a wife?
Do not seek to be free.
Are you free from a wife?
Do not seek a wife.
1 CORINTHIANS 7:27 ESV

Being single and being married both have their blessings. One is not greater than the other, for different ways to serve the Lord are possible with both, and different blessings are associated with each circumstance. Rather than bemoaning what someone else has been called to, try looking at all the Lord has given you in this season and consider how you may use it for his glory.

As believers, we have a responsibility to not sin in our circumstances whether we are married or not. Let's honor the Lord and our spouses by staying faithful to marriage in word, deed, and especially our thoughts.

Lord, thank you for the different seasons we find ourselves in throughout life. Each of them is an opportunity to love you more and serve you better. Please show us how we can serve you now.

SLEEP WELL

It is in vain that you rise up early and go late to rest,
eating the bread of anxious toil;
for he gives to his beloved sleep.

PSALM 127:2 ESV

What are your first feelings when you wake up? How about when you lie down to sleep? Is anxiety eating away at you? You are God's child; your birthright is peace, joy, and eternal security with your Father. Don't let the worries of the world steal your birthright.

Rising early, working hard, and being responsible is very different from striving vainly in our own strength. We can trust God to take care of us while still devoting ourselves to our duties and maintaining a good work ethic. The question is, do you truly trust that God is going to take care of you? If you do, sleep well. He has it under control.

Heavenly Father, we want our first thoughts of the day to be of you and our first feelings to be peaceful. Teach us the balance between working diligently and trusting you. Bless your children's sleep, Lord.

INVESTMENTS

May mercy, peace, and love
be multiplied to you.
JUDE 1:2 NASB

If you are familiar with compound interest, then you know that it is the multiplied return of an investment. Our life in Christ also has a return on our investments, and its compounding profits are mercy, peace, and love.

If we invest in the world, we will reap its flavorless fruit. If we invest in our marriage, it will be stronger and more fulfilling. If we invest in our kids, they will have a more solid foundation as adults. If we invest in God and in understanding his Word, we will reap his rewards, which will be greatly multiplied like any good compound interest. Invest in what matters, not in what diminishes the value of your life. The return is well worth the venture.

There is no better investment we could make than investing our hearts in you, dear Father. Please multiply your mercy, peace, and love back to us and make the most of our lives which we willingly offer to you.

Transparency

Search me, O God, and know my heart;
test me and know my anxious thoughts.

PSALM 139:23 NLT

Even been embarrassed about something you did? Did you hide it because you were scared of the consequences? Maybe you hide things from your spouse because you don't know how they will react. Do you struggle to be transparent about your struggles?

We can bring our sins and fears to God, and they won't overwhelm or surprise him. In fact, he already knows all about them and still loves us unconditionally. He never gives up on us, and he doesn't want us to give up either. He knows the best way to conquer the sin and darkness in our life is to expose it. It's scary, uncomfortable, and humiliating, but darkness is terrified of the light. Bring your anxious thoughts, your hidden sins, the darkness in your heart, your secret struggles, and lay them at the foot of the cross. If they creep back, lay them down again. Ask God and your spouse for help. Whatever you do, live in the light.

Lord, today we will be honest with you, and we will be honest with each other. We want to walk in the light, but we can't do it alone. Search us, dear God.

ALL WE ARE

*Love the LORD your God with all your heart
and with all your soul and with all your strength.*

DEUTERONOMY 6:5 NIV

The Lord has never been interested in a transactional relationship with his people. He has no desire to be one of our hobbies. God, our Creator and salvation, deserves our full attention and passion. Loving our spouses can help us understand the way that God wants us to love him. We love our spouses with affectionate hearts, with our bodies in acts of service and intimacy, and we love them in spirit by encouraging and investing in them.

The Lord asks that our every facet be devoted to him. Our relationship with him should be lively. Much like a marriage, this relationship requires effort. It demands intentionality, honesty, and humility. To love God, and to love a spouse, means loving them with all that we are emotionally, spiritually, and physically.

Lord, awaken our souls to a new depth of relationship with you and with each other. Show us where we lack a fullness of passion and have become apathetic and complacent. We praise you for your bottomless ocean of love, joy, and creativity that allows us to engage our whole selves in relationship with you and each other.

Love Mandate

"This is My commandment,
that you love one another,
just as I have loved you."

John 15:12 NASB

God is love, and he commands us to love like he loves us. Love is not just something we do. It is who we are as children of the God who is love. A husband and wife who love and serve each other are a testimony of what love is supposed to look like.

Love and marriage are not about what we can get; they are about what we can give. Love means giving ourselves; our time, energy, resources, and space, just as God gave so much of himself for us, including his life. Love is not optional for a child of God; his commandment is that we love each other as he has loved us.

Lord, thank you for your example of love. We pray that our marriage can be a testimony of your goodness as we learn to treat each other with love as well.

FAITHFULNESS AND COMPASSION

Be gracious to me, God, according to Your faithfulness;
According to the greatness of Your compassion,
wipe out my wrongdoings.

PSALM 51:1 NASB

Often when we strive for faithfulness, we do it with mumbling and discontent. We will stay married, but not happily. We will stay at our job, but not with a good attitude. The heart of God is in contrast to this, abounding in faithfulness rooted in compassion. He is not faithful to us because he has to be. Out of compassion for our poor souls, he is willing to "wipe out" our wrongdoings. He is not chained to us; he binds himself to people he knows will run away time and time again.

Despite this, he chooses to love anyway. He chooses to invest in us and be gracious to us. This is the image of true Christian marriage: the compassionate, covenant relationship between God and the church. If we want this in our marriage, we will pray for hearts of faithfulness rooted in compassion as well as loyalty.

God, give us hearts of compassion and commitment this day. Make us people of open hearts who are willing to love when unloved and willing to stay true when abandoned.

ADULTERY AND IDOLATRY

*"You shall obey the voice of the LORD your God,
and observe His commandments and His statutes
which I command you today."*
DEUTERONOMY 27:10 NKJV

In the Bible, the relationship between God and his people is often compared to a marriage, and spiritual idolatry is equated with marital infidelity. The bond we have with the Lord is not something to be taken lightly. Sin is a violation of our union with God just as infidelity is a violation of our marriage promise to forsake all others. Our spirits belong to the Lord when we ask him to save us. When we dethrone God in our lives to replace him with another authority, we commit spiritual adultery.

Jesus came to atone for that spiritual adultery, which, as sinful humans, we can't fully put to death until we are glorified. When we fall into spiritual adultery, we feel a righteous shame, but after asking for forgiveness, we feel a deep gratitude for the God who gave us the ability to be forgiven.

Father, please use our marriage to teach us about your desire for our hearts. Help us understand the similarity between adultery and idolatry, and let it move us to be more dedicated to a faithful relationship with you and each other. Thank you for sending Jesus so our shortcomings could be used to further your glory.

GENUINE LOVE

Let love be genuine. Abhor what is evil;
hold fast to what is good.
ROMANS 12:9 ESV

The devil works hard to make sin seem attractive, but if we really understood how deeply hurtful it is to our loving God, we would abhor it. People everywhere try to soft-peddle their sin to appease their guilt, but the truth is that whatever is not for God is against God. Scripture tells us to "hold fast" to what is good because it is not easy. It takes intentionality and dedication.

Genuine love for the Lord and for others motivates us to do what is good and refuse what is evil. We can't fake love; either it will be genuine, or it will be exposed as forced. To genuinely love God, we have to genuinely know God because how can we love someone we don't know? Hold fast to what is good, hold tightly to spending time with God, and evil will become more and more abhorrent to you.

We genuinely love you, Lord, and we want to know you more. When we think of how it hurts your heart to watch your children flirt with evil, it horrifies us. We never want to do that! Please keep us far from evil.

Prayerful Approach

Be anxious for nothing, but in everything by prayer and supplication,
with thanksgiving, let your requests be made known to God; and the
peace of God, which surpasses all understanding, will guard your
hearts and minds through Christ Jesus.

PHILIPPIANS 4:6-7 NKJV

Christian marriage is not devoid of problems, but the difference is we can take issues to Christ in prayer and find help. Instead of feeling anxious and overwhelmed, believers may humbly and gratefully approach God with whatever is on their minds.

Mature prayer includes thanking God for all he has done in addition to asking for his help. We believers don't have problem-free lives and marriages, but we do have the greatest helper on our team ready to lead us through any obstacle. Addressing problems with real, lasting answers begins with prayer because all true wisdom comes from God. Reliance on Christ creates contentment and produces peace in marriage as well as our other relationships.

Lord, sometimes life throws a lot at us, and we don't know how to deal with it. Sometimes our marriage goes through tough times, and we get anxious. We ask, Father, that you guard our hearts and minds against anxiety, give us peace, and strengthen our marriage.

The Greatest Love

"Greater love has no one than this,
than to lay down one's life for his friends."

JOHN 15:13 NKJV

Christ loved and cherished the church, his bride, so dearly that he gave up his life for her. In doing so, he offered the greatest example of love: the innocent willingly sacrificing themselves for the guilty.

Do you love your spouse? Your family? Your friends? Perhaps there is no crucifixion in your future, but Christ made it clear that love is active and not passive. Love is a lifestyle and not feelings or empty words. Every day Jesus served those he met. He washed feet, fed the hungry, healed the hurting, and taught those who were desperate to understand more. Ultimately, he gave himself over to death on our behalf, but he gave up his own life each and every day for the sake of those he loved. That is true, great, unconditional love.

King Jesus, we are in awe of the love you have shown us. Amazingly, you have put this same love in us to pour out on other people. When we're feeling tired or selfish, remind us of your great love and flood our hearts again.

CONFIDENCE IN GOD

Do not throw away this confident trust in the Lord.
Remember the great reward it brings you!
Patient endurance is what you need now,
so that you will continue to do God's will.
Then you will receive all that he has promised.
HEBREWS 10:35-36 NLT

It's tempting to rely on our abilities and resources rather than trust the Lord and depend on his provisions, but we can't serve two masters. It is either us or God. Scripture constantly reminds us to place our trust in the Lord because it turns out much better for us if we do. We can keep pressing on against all odds because we have confidence in God's ability and intention to provide for us.

Let's face today's challenges with courage and confidence. It may take longer than feels comfortable for things to turn around, but with patience and endurance, we will experience the rewards God has promised for those who persevere.

Oh God, sometimes it feels like things will never change. Sometimes it seems there is no way through. In those moments, remind us how great you are and how much you care.

HOPE

Be of good courage,
And He shall strengthen your heart,
All you who hope in the LORD.

PSALM 31:24 NKJV

What happens when hard times fall on you, your family, or your nation? How do you conduct yourself? Look around. You will see people who crumble under pressure, who hide away from uncertainty, who become angry and uncontrollable when threatened, who turn to temporary comfort when subjected to discomfort, and who become depressed or hopeless in the face of loss.

We are not like the world which only hopes in itself. We put our hope in the everlasting, all-powerful King of the universe! Our hope will never be disappointed. The Lord gives us strength and courage to face anything that comes our way.

Mighty King, our hope is in you. Thank you for equipping us with the strength and courage we need to face each day. We are different from the world because of you. Our marriage is different, our family is different, and we shine your light in this dark and despondent generation.

Love Is a Choice

We know what real love is because Jesus gave up his life for us.
So we also ought to give up our lives for our brothers and sisters.
1 John 3:16 NLT

God's love is deep and intimate. His love is sacrificial and acts on our behalf. Love is not a desire for someone else based on personal gratification; it's a desire for someone else's well-being. When someone is willing to put their own needs and romantic satisfaction second to the needs of someone else, that is genuine love.

Love is deeper than its emotion. God's love, as seen through today's verse, is best understood as a choice to act selflessly for someone else. It is the effective, powerful choice of God to look beyond the sins of his people, pay their debt, and forgive them rather than let them perish. If God has such immense love for us, who are nothing compared to him, what sort of love should we have for each other as equals?

Dear God, we love each other because you loved us first. As your blood watered the earth at the foot of the cross, it brought salvation to those who pray in your name. Today, we will walk in your love and treat others with the self-sacrificing mercy you first showed to us.

EVERYTHING IN LOVE

*Let all that you do
be done with love.*

1 CORINTHIANS 16:14 NKJV

Throughout his letter to the Corinthians, Paul gave several practical admonitions and encouragements for those who desired to live in a way that honored the Lord. Paul wanted the believers in Corinth to grow in their Christian faith and walk in spirit and truth. Refusing to shy away from difficult subjects, he tackled issues dividing the church and exposed the foolishness of human wisdom by contrasting it with the wisdom of God. He laid out principles for marriage and godly conduct, discussed the importance of the Lord's Supper, and explained the kinds of spiritual gifts. The point of it all? Love.

Paul's teaching pointed to the supremacy of love over everything else. This is how our mindset of marriage, and life as a whole, should be.

Lord, thank you for the love you show us which teaches us to love as well. May everything we do, say, and think be out of the love you freely gave to us.

No Plan B

*"You will seek Me and find Me
when you search for Me with all your heart."*
JEREMIAH 29:13 NASB

When you pray, do you imagine that God is standing by and ready to take your order like a waiter? Or do you understand that he is King on his throne, welcoming you with open arms? He wants you to seek him before all else. Before you'd married your spouse, if they had told you that you were their plan B after trying someone else first, would you have felt loved?

Well, God is no different. He has no intention of being anyone's plan B or sharing his throne with other gods in your life. There is no room for half-hearted Christians in his perfect plan. Humbly and sincerely, let's lay our other dreams and gods down before him and search for him with our whole hearts.

With our whole hearts, Lord, we seek you today. You are more important than our schedules, friends, bank accounts, and everything else in our lives. We submit everything to you today.

COMMUNITY

Whoever says he is in the light and hates his brother is still in darkness.
Whoever loves his brother abides in the light,
and in him there is no cause for stumbling.
1 JOHN 2:9-10 ESV

When you encounter trouble and hardship, isn't it reassuring to have someone you can count on? Usually, the person you can count on is the closest person to you: your spouse. But what about when you both need help? This is why community is so important and why God designed us to be part of a bigger body of believers.

Living in community is often difficult simply because there are more people. Conflict arises, and it's easier to avoid it than work through it. Hate can creep in, and suddenly we are thrown into darkness. Still, the work is worth it when it comes to relationships: your relationship with the Lord, your spouse, and the community God has given you. Life is richer and more rewarding when filled with relationships and love.

Your design is perfect, dear God, and you designed us for relationships. Thank you for our marriage, our brothers and sisters in Christ, and most of all for our relationship with you.

LOYALTY AND KINDNESS

Never let loyalty and kindness leave you!
Tie them around your neck as a reminder.
Write them deep within your heart.

PROVERBS 3:3 NLT

If you have someone in your life who is loyal and kind even under pressure and in dark days, hold tightly to that person. That is a friendship worth keeping close. Marriage is a friendship meant to last a lifetime, and nobody wants to be tied to an unkind person. Exercise loyalty and practice kindness.

Anyone can be loyal and kind when it's mutually beneficial and life is good, but what about when it's tough? What about when you're angry, or you're tempted, or your spouse isn't being kind? There is a reason the Bible uses extreme imagery like "tie them around your neck" and "write them deep within your heart." It won't always be easy, yet those are the moments that matter and make the biggest difference in a relationship. Hold fast!

You have never left us, Lord, and your kindness is unwavering. Help us be more like you in the way we treat each other and all our other relationships.

HUMBLY FAITHFUL

Peter said to him, "Lord, why can I not follow you now?
I will lay down my life for you."
JOHN 13:37 ESV

A faithful person is dependable. They bring a sense of security and peace to those who rely on them. It is good for us to be men and women of our word so others know they can trust us. This is especially important within marriage because of the high level of trust needed to have an intimate relationship.

Ultimately, only God is faithful all the time. Even with the best intentions, like Peter, we all fail sometimes. Peter failed terribly, and his story of unfaithfulness stands as a stark warning for us as well as a glorious example of God's grace. Rather than grow cocky in our good intentions or rely heavily on our own merit, let's look to Jesus' example of faithfulness and use his strength. He has generously gifted it to us.

How desperately we want to promise to stay faithful to you, Lord God! Peter's wake-up call is a heartbreaking story, and we want to learn from that rather than experience it ourselves. Please, God, give us your strength to remain true to you, to each other, and to anyone who relies on us.

God's Mighty Hand

Humble yourselves under the mighty hand of God, that He may exalt you in due time, casting all your care upon Him, for He cares for you.

1 Peter 5:6-7 NKJV

God cares for you! Is that hard to believe sometimes? When the hand of God weighs heavily on us, like it did on Job as he lay in the dust, how can we believe God cares for us? How can we cast our anxieties on a God who seems harsh in the measures of his love?

This is what it means to die to ourselves and live for Christ. The choice to humble ourselves under the hand of God is the choice to love God. That love, born in the fires of difficulty, lives on in times of peace. Our love for God comes from our choice to trust him rather than rely on ourselves. The love we have for our spouses similarly comes from our love for God. Our choice to humble ourselves gives birth to more love and is made manifest when we are exalted from difficulty.

Lord of love and God of our tribulation, give us the faith to cast every anxiety on you when we are tempted by pain and sorrow to resent you instead. Use this trial to sow seeds of deep, everlasting love in our hearts.

THE EXTRA MILE

"If someone slaps you on one cheek, turn to them the other also. If someone takes your coat, do not withhold your shirt from them. Give to everyone who asks you, and if anyone takes what belongs to you, do not demand it back. Do to others as you would have them do to you."

LUKE 6:29-31 NIV

This passage appears counterproductive or even dangerous at face value. Who wants to turn the other cheek when slapped? Most of us would feel the urge to retaliate. The point Jesus was making wasn't to allow yourself to be abused or become a passive participant in violence; it's about going the extra mile.

Let's go above and beyond what is expected of us because that is how Jesus lived. In marriage, we will face times when we must go the extra mile, not because we were compelled or forced, but because of our great love and devotion for Jesus.

Lord, you tell us to turn our cheek, give our coat, and go the extra mile. Honestly, God, we often don't feel like doing that, but we know faith is tested and love is proven in those actions. Please help us be strong when those moments arise. Thank you.

LIVING FOR GOD

*God is not unjust; he will not forget your work and the love you have
shown him as you have helped his people and continue to help them.*
HEBREWS 6:10 NIV

Regardless of our station in life, God is the one ultimately judging
all we do, so all our services are really for him. From the mistreated,
enslaved person to the wealthiest leader, everyone is called to work
for God's honor and glory.

Although it seems unfair how much some people have and how
little others have, that is a temporary way of thinking because God
has a specific calling for each of us. Our life on earth is short, and
the best we can do is use however much or little we have received
in service to our King. God asks us to love him by loving and
serving his people. How can you love him today? How can you love
your spouse? How can you use the position you have been given
and the resources you have in service to God?

Lord, everything we have and all that we are is for your
glory. Our positions, our money, our marriage, and our
whole lives are for you. Show us how we can love you
today by loving others.

FINDING THE ONE

Hardly had I left them
When I found him whom my soul loves;
I held on to him and would not let him go.
SONG OF SOLOMON 3:4 NASB

Lots of single people who long for a partner would love to know who they will end up marrying. This wish is understandable because marriage is one of the most important life decisions a person can make. Choosing a lifelong partner is not something to take lightly, and for believers it requires a lot of prayer and guidance from God and from his Word.

In the Song of Solomon verse today, we can see the value that the young lady has put on her fiancé; she will not let go of him until she is properly married to him. She sees his worth and holds him in high regard. How can we value our spouses?

Lord, help us value each other as we did when we first started our relationship. Help us not to lose that first spark or the deep feelings we have for each other as we grow together in your love.

Bigger Picture

We know that in all things God works for the good of those who love him, who have been called according to his purpose.
ROMANS 8:28 NIV

Following Christ does not mean things will go smoothly all the time. It does mean that, as cliché as it sounds, everything will definitely work together for good. We don't always get to see what this "good" is; God doesn't work on our schedule. On the last day, we will see all good come to fruition.

The journey of faith is not for the faint-hearted. Praise God we are never alone! He upholds us. If your path today is grim, trust in the one who has a perfect bird's-eye view. He can see the bigger picture that we can't even imagine.

Mighty God, the road often feels long and difficult, but we know how much more difficult life would be without you. You give us love, peace, joy, and strength to carry on; you hold all our tears. You will work out everything for our good and your glory.

February

God created mankind in his own image,

in the image of God he created them;

male and female he created them.

GENESIS 1:27 NIV

EVER STRONGER

Be truly glad. There is wonderful joy ahead, even though you must endure many trials for a little while. These trials will show that your faith is genuine. It is being tested as fire tests and purifies gold—though your faith is far more precious than mere gold. So when your faith remains strong through many trials, it will bring you much praise and glory and honor on the day when Jesus Christ is revealed to the whole world.

1 PETER 1:6-7 NLT

The paradox of our faith is that we can rejoice in our suffering and distress. The mystery of our call to glory is that we can celebrate our freedom in Christ while subject to terrible trials and losses. The reason these impossibilities are real is because we have an unfailing hope in our eternal inheritance and the glorious redemption of our bodies through Jesus Christ our Lord.

In marriage, tough times will come, and how we walk through them will greatly influence the strength of our union together and with God. Hardships can rupture a relationship or bind it closer. Whatever you are facing, find God's peace and joy in the midst of it, and you will come through it stronger than ever.

Dear Lord, thank you for the gift of life and opportunity found amidst difficulty. Thank you for seeing us through life's challenges and filling us with your joy every single day.

ENDURING LOVE

Give thanks to the God of heaven.
His faithful love endures forever.
PSALM 136:26 NLT

Who is in a better position to make a promise of forever than God? As the Creator of all, with a perfect record of upholding every promise he's ever made, the Lord is the most qualified entity to teach us what love and devotion mean.

As we lean into God's love and learn from his Scriptures, let's give thanks to God through prayer and praise but most of all through loving other people. This is what God desires most: that we love him and love others. How can we show God how much we love him by living out our gratefulness in loving our spouse?

Oh God of heaven, we give you thanks today and every day for your enduing love and your faithfulness forever.

HEART OF MERCY

He heals the brokenhearted
and binds up their wounds.
PSALM 147:3 NIV

Love is one of the most beautiful things in our world. One of its beautiful expressions is in compassion, which is why the Bible often explains love in the context of loving the poor. God expresses his love by binding up the wounds of the brokenhearted and healing their afflictions. These acts overflow with mercy and majesty, and they demand our respect and attention.

When we think of love, this is what we should picture. Love is the decision to put someone else's needs ahead of our own. When that person is in dire need or hurt, that love is all the more beautiful. When we commit our hearts to this form of love, we will find that our commitment to a spouse flows naturally. Being committed to love means being committed to God's plan of redemption and restoration.

Gracious and loving Lord Jesus, give us love. Give us the kind of love that genuinely cares about the wellness of others and for the brokenhearted. May our actions flow from a selfless sentiment of love.

ETERNAL LOVE

Love never ends. As for prophecies, they will pass away;
as for tongues, they will cease; as for knowledge, it will pass away.
1 CORINTHIANS 13:8 ESV

Love never fails because love is eternal. Selfless love will continue spread throughout the people of the Lord forever. Examples of selfless love in the present are mere glimpses of the normal state of eternity. Even spiritual gifts of prophecy, tongues, and knowledge will, as Paul pronounces, all pass away. Why? Because when Christ returns and all is made right, we no longer will need them.

Love, however, will remain forever. God's love and our reflection of it to each other will go on endlessly. What an epic overlay to God's design for marriage: the love between a husband and wife is a glimpse into the love we will experience forever with our Lord and Savior.

Lord Jesus, we are in awe of your everlasting love which continues when all else fails. Thank you for the gift of marriage in which we can love and be loved. It gives us a taste of the incredible, lasting, loving union you have arranged between you and your bride forever.

Plugged In

Just as each of us has one body with many members, and these members do not all have the same function, so in Christ we, though many, form one body, and each member belongs to all the others.
ROMANS 12:4-5 NIV

Are you plugged in to a local community of believers? Our awesome Creator made us to work together as a body and not as separate entities. We each have an important part to play. We have a role in marriage, our family, our church, and within our circle of friends. Our distinct roles, when combined together to use our differences and strengths, make for a healthier body as a whole. We are part of something bigger than ourselves.

Where is God calling you to plug in today? What part can you serve?

Heavenly Father, thank you for giving us the pleasure of a brand-new day full of hope, joy, and love for each other. Thank you for showing us the way. Teach us through your Scriptures that we are all one, and may we live in unity and harmony in your Son, Jesus Christ.

SELFLESS

No one is to seek his own advantage,
but rather that of his neighbor.
1 CORINTHIANS 10:24 NASB

Marriage is not about what is fair. Our relationship between us and God is not fair; anyone who has children knows their relationship with them is not fair; rarely are friendships completely fair either.

There is no room for self-centeredness in marriage, especially between Christians who have submitted to a life of following Christ's example of sacrificial love. It is our duty and opportunity to serve our spouses and look for ways to bless them. Seeking our own advantage in a relationship is a great way to squash growth and limit love.

Father, forgive us. We are often selfish and fail to think through the implications of our decisions and how they will affect others. We want to be like you in love and service. Please help us as we learn to approach our relationships with grace and patience.

GOD'S PLANS

"I know the plans I have for you," declares the LORD,
"plans to prosper you and not to harm you,
plans to give you hope and a future."
JEREMIAH 29:11 NIV

Have you ever wished for something intensely only to realize, after you got it, that it was not nearly as great as you thought it would be? God's gifts are not like that. They are unbelievably satisfying, exciting, and engaging.

Looking back on your life, do you feel you have missed opportunities or come short of where you thought you would be by now? What gauge are you using: heaven's or earth's? Our plans are not God's plans because God has a much greater imagination! He wants to show and tell us things that we couldn't comprehend without him enlightening us. Are you ready to let go of your mediocre dreams in exchange for God's prosperous plans?

Oh Lord, we surrender our dreams, wishes, desires, and plans to your better ways. Please lead us on your path.

ACCESSIBLE

This High Priest of ours understands our weaknesses, for he faced all of the same testings we do, yet he did not sin. So let us come boldly to the throne of our gracious God. There we will receive his mercy, and we will find grace to help us when we need it most.

HEBREWS 4:15-16 NLT

Our confidence to approach God in prayer is not based on our own merit but on that of Jesus Christ. Nothing we have done allows us to boldly go before God; it's what Jesus did for us on the cross. Because of him, we know we are washed clean, declared innocent, set free, and given access to Almighty God.

Isn't it a relief to know we can go to God any time we need his help and mercy because our great High Priest, Jesus Christ, stood in the gap for us? The grace shown to us is truly unfathomable. In response, let us be quick to run to God whenever we need help, and may we be happy to show grace to others.

We confidently come before you today, God, not because we have earned the right but because you have declared us innocent. Thank you for paying the price for our sins on our behalf. May we never undermine your sacrifice on the cross by carrying around guilt which no longer belongs to us.

HOLD TIGHT

Show love to the LORD your God by walking in his ways and holding tightly to him.

DEUTERONOMY 11:22 NLT

Have you ever been to a garage sale and seen a stash of precious jewels dumped in the one-dollar box? That would be huge shock! We hold on to things of value. We treasure heirlooms and photographs that remind us of loved ones or cherished memories. We keep our valuables in a safe place and not strewn about. Right?

How valuable is the Lord to you? Do you hold on tightly to your relationship with him? The children of Israel were instructed to hold on to the law of God tightly because it was of great value. How close do you hold your marriage? Your family and friends? Your health? What we value, we will protect and keep close.

We love you with all our hearts, Lord God, and we want to walk in your ways. We will protect our time with you and hold your statutes close. We will also love and cling to each other. Our marriage matters, and it was a gift to us from you.

WISDOM

Blessed is the one who finds wisdom,
and the one who gets understanding,
for the gain from her is better than gain from silver
and her profit better than gold.

PROVERBS 3:13-14 ESV

We sweat and toil to make a buck, but how much effort to we put into seeking wisdom? Wisdom is worth much more, and it's far easier to obtain, yet we spend most of our lives trying to earn an income.

While we need to work to put food on the table, even more vital to our well-being is the spiritual food that only God can supply. Let's not become so engulfed in figuring out our next physical meal that we starve ourselves spiritually. Wisdom is found with God, and by spending time with God, we learn to be wise. The gain far outweighs any treasure here on earth. Are you seeking God daily? Are you helping your spouse find undistracted time to seek God as well?

Lord, we need you more than we need food, air, and sleep, and you know that we also need those things. Please give us what we need so we can give you the best of ourselves.

TROUBLE AND HARDSHIP

Who shall separate us from the love of Christ?
Shall trouble or hardship or persecution or famine
or nakedness or danger or sword?
ROMANS 8:35 NIV

God feels our pain when we undergo hard experiences. He feels the hurt, yet he allows us to pass through them anyway. These troubles exist to prove to us that no matter our external circumstances, the circumstances of our heart remain the same; God's love is there for us. He is dedicated to us even when we sin against him, and he is dedicated to us when we are dismayed and persecuted.

God's love does not fade, but our understanding of it is subject to change. Through every hardship, our prayer should be that we more deeply understand the care and devotion God has for us. Our love for our spouses should mirror God's love in its faithfulness. Whether our spouses ignore, annoy, or hurt us, our love for them should still stand. We can demonstrate our commitment to them through our unconditional love for them.

God, give us today the unconditional, unbreakable love of your own heart. Make us strong in commitment, reliable in faithfulness, and unchanging in our dedication to you. Thank you, Lord. Thank you for your unwavering and ever-reliable love for us.

CHILDREN

I have no greater joy than this,
to hear of my children walking in the truth.
3 JOHN 1:4 NASB

Whether you have your own children or you are involved in the lives of other children, being used by God to instill truth and love into others who look up to us is one of the most rewarding assignments we can receive. It may be a grueling, tedious calling at times, but the fruit is eternal.

Whether you are parents, teachers, youth pastors, aunts and uncles, missionaries, or you simply have friends who have children, consider your impact in their lives and do not take your role lightly. The seeds you plant in their lives will be watered and grow. Watch and see what God does!

Oh God of truth, give us your eyes to see the eternal importance of the role you have given us. You love children! We want that same love and respect for children too. May the children looking up to us see a glimpse of you. We want to faithfully share your love and truth.

GOD'S DIRECTIONS

*I reach out for your commands, which I love,
that I may meditate on your decrees.*
PSALM 119:48 NIV

The Lord has given us a set of laws to live by, and they offer guidance to every area of life. The world can be confusing, often challenging our ethics and questioning our commitment, but we have the Holy Spirit to lead us and the Word of God to give us direction.

Many people hear of God's commandments and imagine a legalistic, perfectionistic dictator, but that is not who God is. The commandments are for our benefit, and they were created out of love. God knows that without a firm, parental hand, we would veer off course and into our own demise. He loves us enough to hold us to a higher standard than the passing ways of this world. Reach out for God's commandments; fall in love with them. They are your lifeline and light in a dark world.

Dear Lord, we don't want to misunderstand your commandments or take your Word for granted. Thank you for the directions you have given us. They have richly blessed every aspect of our lives, including our marriage. Please hide your Word in our hearts so we may always know what to do and which way to go.

WEAKNESS AND STRENGTH

Accept the one whose faith is weak,
without quarreling over disputable matters.
ROMANS 14:1 NIV

Most people don't want to be seen as weak. They would rather be considered strong, independent, anything but weak. Especially when it comes to our spirit, we prefer to identify with strength. In this verse, it feels wrong to consider others' faith as weak. Surely it would be wrong to treat them differently because of it. Still, that is what God requires. He does not want us to focus on them as a weak person, but as a person with weakness. Our actions should come from a desire to encourage and bring peace.

If our main takeaway from this verse is to consider ourselves strong and others weak, we miss the point. The point is acceptance, kindness, and the ability to not quarrel. Within our marriages, we often want to root out wrongness in our spouses at every opportunity. We see they hold a wrong opinion, and we confront them about it. We disagree with them on a minor point, and we push to make our own voice heard. This verse from Paul is for times like these.

Lord, take away the quarreling spirit from our hearts. Make us acceptant and wise.

WORTHY LIVING

I, the prisoner of the Lord, urge you to walk in a manner
worthy of the calling with which you have been called.
EPHESIANS 4:1 NASB

As believers, we reflect what or whom we profess as truth, and this applies to our marriages too. Our marriages should glorify God. How we relate to each other and how we treat each other as married people must reflect the faith we profess. Marriage is part of the ministry that is our lives, and it impacts the world around us. This is especially true in a time when marriage has become more of an afterthought than a lifelong commitment.

The verse tells us that we should walk in a way worthy of the calling we have received. Marriage reflects Christ and the church. The lost world needs to see what real love looks and acts like, and Christian marriage is that voice that the world needs to hear.

Lord, thank you for giving us love and forgiveness. Thank you for calling us and redeeming us for your glory. Please enable us to live lives worthy of the calling of our marriages.

UNSPEAKABLE PEACE

May the Lord of peace himself give you peace at all times
and in every way. The Lord be with all of you.

2 THESSALONIANS 3:16 NIV

Are you at peace? What brings you worry and steals your peace? Have you spent time with the Prince of Peace lately? He's happy to refresh you and take away your worries if you ask. His peace is all-encompassing and isn't subject to the daily news. His peace can bring us rest and contentment even when life is falling apart around us. Testimonies of this peace are the Christians who face terrible persecution and even death, yet they still sing his praises with unbreakable joy.

The devil does not have the authority to take your peace; he can only try to trick you into giving it to him. Do not fall for his lies! Do not relinquish your peace. The Lord is with you always.

We pray for your peace, King Jesus. Please flood our hearts with your peace, and may it pour into our marriage, community, country, and world.

GRATITUDE

The generous soul will be made rich,
And he who waters will also be watered himself.
PROVERBS 11:25 NKJV

When we live with gratitude and thankfulness, we find more reasons to be thankful. All generosity is born out of gratitude, for no one can give without acknowledging they have enough. The most generous are the most grateful; they understand how much they've been blessed and want to bless others in turn.

When we are generous with others, we find they are a greater blessing to us because of it. The passage says, "he who waters will also be watered." By pouring ourselves out for others, we create the trust and desire in them to bless us in return. Within marriage, this reciprocity plays out in numerous ways. When we are gracious and forgiving with our spouse, they often return the gesture. In essence, if we water them, like watering a plant, they will grow stronger and have the resources to water us in return.

Dear God, teach us to be generous souls. Fill us with gratitude and grace so those around us might consider us a blessing.

LOVE DEBT

*Owe no one anything except to love one another,
for he who loves another has fulfilled the law.*
ROMANS 13:8 NKJV

Most of us don't like being in debt. Owing someone can hang over our heads like a dark cloud, so it's good (and biblical) to settle our debts when we can.

The Bible talks about a love debt, which is the expectation that we love one another. It's possible that all our earthly debts could be cleared, but we will never be able to repay our love debt. Christ showed us insurmountable love by wiping clean the slate of our sin. All he asks for in return is that we love others on his behalf. Because his great sacrifice can never be fully repaid, we will always owe this love debt, which is exactly what Christ intended.

King Jesus, we owe you everything. The currency you request from us is love, and its recipients are other people. Please help us extend love to all who need it according to your perfect will.

Motivation

*Let us think of ways to motivate one another
to acts of love and good works.*

Hebrews 10:24 nlt

As members of a greater body of believers and as citizens of the kingdom of God, we have a bigger role to play than simply being concerned for our own well-being. We are instructed to help our brothers and sisters in Christ and look for ways to bless them and motivate them toward love and good works. We are to care for each other because God cares for us.

Marriage is a fantastic way to involve ourselves in this because we are handed opportunities every day to love, encourage, motivate, bless, and care for our spouse. When our marriage is strong, even more opportunities open up for us to influence the world around us together. How are you going to love, encourage, and motivate your spouse today?

Heavenly Father, thank you for those who encouraged and motivated us to press forward to what you have called us to do. We also want to be that blessing in the lives of others; please give us opportunities to do so. May we be in tune with you so others move toward lives of love and good works through our witness.

BY GOD'S GRACE

By the grace of God I am what I am, and his grace toward me was not in vain. On the contrary, I worked harder than any of them, though it was not I, but the grace of God that is with me.

1 CORINTHIANS 15:10 ESV

Have you ever worked in a place that had a "best practice" or "standard practice?" It is a vetted way of doing something that has been proven, over time, through trial and error, and by many participants, to be the safest and most efficient way of performing the work.

Christians understand that our best practice for living and loving is to follow God's model. This isn't founded only in stubborn religious adherence. It has thousands of years of trial and error by many, many participants. God's grace is with us, and that helps us accomplish what God has laid on our hearts. The best way is going to be his way. That's not blind faith; it's vetted confidence.

Lord, we know you hold all things together, and in you we find perfection, ability, direction, purpose, and worth. By you and because of you, we are overjoyed to serve you with all we are and all we have.

CONFIDENT HOPE

I pray that God, the source of hope, will fill you completely with joy and peace because you trust in him. Then you will overflow with confident hope through the power of the Holy Spirit.

ROMANS 15:13 NLT

It's great to think about eternity, but that's then and this is now. Daily life can be difficult. We need God's hope, joy, and peace to make it through. While those attributes sound nice, what does it mean to practically apply them to our everyday grind?

First and foremost, we need to trust Christ. No matter what is happening around us, we know that our Lord within us will preserve and protect us through everything. Believing this will give us hope and confidence. Hope gives motivation to continue. Confidence is contagious. Have you seen timid people become inspired when someone more confident tries first? Picture a couple kids at the top of a giant waterslide or an army after a general's pre-battle speech. When we're confident that God will take care of us, it overflows to other people.

Teach us to trust you, Lord. We place our hope in you. Please fill us with confidence so others will see how trustworthy you are and also place their trust in you.

OUR BEST LIFE

What does the LORD your God ask of you but to fear the LORD your God,
to walk in obedience to him, to love him, to serve the LORD your God
with all your heart and with all your soul?

DEUTERONOMY 10:12 NIV

Our Father wants us to have life. He created the garden of Eden to be a place of communion with his people. We see this Eden theme sprinkled throughout the Bible when God's people obey him. When the people of Israel followed the law, they experienced victory in war, peace in their city, and great fruitfulness.

God knows how our lives can honor him, and he has given us the Bible and his Holy Spirit to teach us how to live it. God's way is good and leads to peace and communion with him. By submitting to his instruction, we experience the good he desires to give us. In a perfect, sinless world, we wouldn't lose sight of God's will for us, but this side of eternity, we have to struggle with our sinful natures that tell us we can figure out life on our own.

Lord, thank you for guiding us and giving us your Word. Without your instruction, our lives would fall apart. Please speak to us and show us how to live and honor you.

Public Progress

Be diligent in these matters; give yourself wholly to them,
so that everyone may see your progress.
1 TIMOTHY 4:15 NIV

The best way to not fail is to not try. Making mistakes in front of others can be humiliating and frightening, but that is the way to learn and grow. Our perfect God does not demand perfection from us; he took care of our mistakes and imperfections on the cross. He wants us to be diligent with the matters at hand.

Has he given you a task? Throw yourself into it and allow others to see your progress however messy it may be. Has he given you a husband or wife to love? Love them as best as you can. When you mess up, sincerely apologize. When you misunderstand them, seek clarity and try again. Who benefits when you become defensive or cover up your errors? Just be diligent and genuine.

Gracious God, thank you for the job you have given us to do and thank you for giving us spouses to love. Be merciful to us as we walk in our humanity and learn from our mistakes.

GUARD YOUR MOUTH

One who guards his mouth and his tongue,
Guards his soul from troubles.
PROVERBS 21:23 NASB

How often have your words gotten you into trouble? A person who holds complete control over their speech is rare. Perhaps you recently insulted your husband or wife either on purpose or accidentally. Our words are like fire: they can offer great warmth and encouragement, or they can bring massive destruction. Words should not be thrown around carelessly.

How can we avoid trouble by reining in our tongues? It requires humility, self-control, awareness, and a whole lot of prayer. As messengers and ambassadors of God, we need to train our tongues and guard our mouths. What we say may have a greater impact for either good or evil than we realize.

Please guard our mouths, Lord Jesus, and teach us to use our words wisely. We want our speech to be edifying to you and encouraging to others. We invite you into our relationship. Help us, as a couple, always build each other up and not tear each other down.

Humble Love

Always be humble and gentle. Be patient with each other,
making allowance for each other's faults because of your love.

Ephesians 4:2 nlt

If you have been married for any amount of time, you know your spouse has faults, and they know you have them too. Being married as imperfect partners can easily result in grudges, resentment, and a general dislike for each other, but that is not what God wants for your marriage. Not to mention it sounds miserable!

Failure to show humility and gentleness to each other in our weaknesses can lead to strife which makes marriages fail, churches split, and friends begrudgingly part ways. Making allowances for people does not mean excusing sin, but it does mean we should show grace because God showed us grace. When your spouse is irritating or coming short of your expectations, how can you remain humble and loving while showing them grace and patience?

Oh God, please help us when we are angry and irritated at each other. Humble us by bringing to mind the countless times you have shown us grace. Remind us of how much you love us so we can love each other even better.

CHANGING CIRCUMSTANCES

In everything give thanks;
for this is the will of God in Christ Jesus for you.
1 THESSALONIANS 5:18 NKJV

Whether you have a good week or a bad week, you have the same God who uses all circumstances for your growth and his glory. God does not change. Our circumstances, however, are constantly changing.

Although we may not feel grateful during difficult seasons, we still have all the reasons imaginable to give God thanks. He is still on the throne, still redeeming the lost, still blessing the faithful, and still loving us unconditionally regardless of whether it's sunny or raining. Find that thanksgiving deep in your heart; it's rooted in something more timeless that your current circumstances. This is what God wants for us.

We will praise you in good times and bad, Lord God. Even if everything else changes, you don't change. We know we can lean on you. Thank you for being always faithful and always loving.

FRUITFUL

"I am the vine, you are the branches.
He who abides in Me, and I in him, bears much fruit;
for without Me you can do nothing."
JOHN 15:5 NKJV

A fruitful life and marriage are desirable, but the only way they happen is if we're plugged in to the source of growth. A branch can't produce fruit by lying on the ground by itself. If we want a healthy, thriving marriage, it's going to require some plugging in and some pruning.

Spend time with God and cut out what is stunting your growth. Pruning is necessary to cultivate the fruit of the Spirit: "Love, joy, peace, patience, kindness, goodness, faithfulness, gentleness, and self-control" (Gal. 5:22-23). Would this fruit create a marriage you would want to be part of? It doesn't happen without spending time with God and trimming anything that goes against him.

Without you, God, we can do nothing. Without you, our marriage and our lives would be devoid of so much goodness. You offer us many gifts in abundance. All you ask for is that we abide with you, and we want to forever. Please nourish the fruit of your Spirit in us.

BEING SURE

Jesus said to him, "No one, having put his hand to the plow, and looking back, is fit for the kingdom of God."
LUKE 9:62 NKJV

The Bible speaks many times about indecisiveness or double-mindedness, and it's not flattering. Nobody likes an indecisive person in a marriage. Marriage is a decisive commitment where two people choose one path over another. In this choice, the path of singleness is forsaken, and the path of partnership is accepted for a lifetime. Both people count the cost of their decision and then lay down their selfish desires in order to serve the needs of the other person.

The commitment professed in marriage vows also applies to the Christian walk. Jesus says that an indecisive believer is really not a believer at all. Commitment in faith and marriage are similar because no person should enter either one without being fully engaged.

Lord, your Word tells us to not be double-minded or indecisive in our walk with you. This also applies to the union of marriage. Both are acts of full commitment. Indecisiveness is an avenue Satan can use to sow discord and stagnation in marriage. Please keep us resolute and focused and put your guidance into our marriage.

MARCH

Place me like a seal over your heart,

like a seal on your arm.

For love is as strong as death,

its jealousy as enduring as the grave.

SONG OF SOLOMON 8:6 NLT

TEMPTATION

Let no one say when he is tempted, "I am tempted by God";
for God cannot be tempted by evil, nor does He Himself tempt anyone.
JAMES 1:13 NKJV

There is a huge difference between temptation and a test of faith. Temptation entices you to sin. It is a scheme of the devil. God, however, will offer you tests to grow your faith. They will not be laced with evil desires and threats of sin; they will be opportunities for a higher level of living and a way to put your faith into action.

For the sake of your soul and your marriage, please, dear Christian, do not dabble in temptation! Do not fool yourself into believing you can withstand the devil and his wiles without the presence of God. Only the Lord can defeat the devil. We must stick close to him and not give temptation a second glance.

Lord God, when this world tempts us, give us the wisdom, strength, and determination to turn away from it. We want to honor you as well as our marriage.

RESPONDING TO MERCY

*I urge you, brothers and sisters, in view of God's mercy,
to offer your bodies as a living sacrifice, holy and pleasing to God—
this is your true and proper worship.*

ROMANS 12:1 NIV

How remarkable is God's mercy? Have you taken time to ponder all the ways he has been merciful to us? If so, it begs the question: what is an appropriate response from us in the knowledge of his great mercy?

Writing to the Roman Christians, Paul explained that true worship is offering ourselves in service to God as if we were living sacrifices for him. Our purpose is for his praise and worship. What better purpose could there be? We get the honor of living for something beyond this temporary existence and greater than ourselves. God granted us mercy so we could be part of his great work on the earth. What a generous gift and calling!

Oh God, thank you for showing us the mercy we desperately need. We commit ourselves, our marriage, our careers, our family, and every other aspect of our lives to you today.

Never Unanswered

*I love the Lord, because he has heard my voice
and my pleas for mercy.
Because he inclined his ear to me,
therefore I will call on him as long as I live.*

Psalm 116:1-2 esv

Silence is a painful thing. Most people can't handle it from their spouse for long, and few Christians can handle it well from their Savior. In times of doubt and questioning, we want to hear the voice of God, and that is a good desire. The psalmist in today's verse is rejoicing because he has heard the word of God, and his desperate pleas have been answered. He is no longer in doubt and anguish but in the comfort of knowing God's answer.

God also uses silence to grow our faith. He withholds his voice at times to test us and mold us into strong, resilient children of God. God also restrains his voice to remind us of his unconditional and unchanging promise; we are in his family as long as we confess him as lord and believe in him. No matter the silence, no matter the waiting, God's promise to us never changes.

God, work in our hearts to produce steadfast patience. In spiritually dry spells, remind us that your commitment to us never changes. We always have the unconditional promise of your love and salvation.

SPIRIT AGAINST FLESH

Walk by the Spirit, and you will not carry out the desire of the flesh.
For the desire of the flesh is against the Spirit, and the Spirit against the
flesh; for these are in opposition to one another, in order to keep you
from doing whatever you want. But if you are led by the Spirit,
you are not under the Law.

GALATIANS 5:16-18 NASB

When the children of Israel entered the Promised Land, many entrenched enemies occupied the hills of Canaan. The Jewish people had to fight for every inch of it, and then they had to fight to keep what they conquered.

This is a picture of the Christian life. There is victory to be had, but it will not come easily or quickly. We are at war with our flesh which doesn't want to yield. There is no reprieve from this struggle, and that's why it takes so long for us to grow. This is the process of sanctification. For this reason, we have to depend on the Spirit of God to overcome the works of the flesh in us.

Heavenly Father, thank you for giving us a regenerated spirit and the power to live in spirit and truth. We know that this strength comes from you, and we praise you for your correction. May we learn to not succumb to desires of the flesh but rather walk in newness of life.

INFLUENCE

Blessed is the one who does not walk in step with the wicked
or stand in the way that sinners take
or sit in the company of mockers,
but whose delight is in the law of the LORD,
and who meditates on his law day and night.

PSALM 1:1-2 NIV

The people we surround ourselves with have a great influence on our lives whether we notice it or not. The words we hear regularly and the attitudes demonstrated by those we spend time with have a significant impact on us. The phrase "you are what you eat" gets the point across; the things we put into our bodies (or lives) have a visible effect on us. This is why the author of this passage emphasized choosing friends wisely. If we choose friends who reject truth and righteousness, regardless of our pure intentions, we will have a near-impossible time remaining on solid ground.

Familiarity is a strong influence; we gravitate toward what we know, so we have to pay attention to what, and whom, we are allowing to influence us. First and foremost, our influence should be coming from God through prayer and Scripture. Beyond that, we should seek relationships with people who are more spiritually mature than ourselves who can speak truth to us and correct us in love.

Lord God, we are often blind to the influences we allow into our lives. Please convict us of choices we have made that pull us away from you. Show us how we can recommit to filling our time and space with relationships that honor you.

APPROVED WORKER

*Do your best to present yourself to God as one approved, a worker who
has no need to be ashamed, rightly handling the word of truth.*
2 TIMOTHY 2:15 ESV

Marriage takes deliberate work. Anything worthwhile requires
personal effort or cost. Many people naively think their marriage
will succeed without the level of effort other marriages seem
to require. They may believe their relationship will function
automatically without spending time on love, compatibility, and
communication. Relationships, especially marriages, don't work
that way.

Marriage is a beautiful creation given to us by God to enhance
our lives, but it has to be cultivated, worked, and nurtured like
any other living thing. You pour into your spouse, and they pour
into you. You are both responsible for this living relationship. In 2
Timothy 2:15, we read that as believers, we present ourselves to
God as approved workers. Similarly, we work to show that we value
our spouses and marriages.

Lord, thank you for the gift of marriage and for the
work you do in us to perfect us. We strive to be better
spouses and teammates. Please help us put in the
effort needed to make our marriage work long-term for
your glory. Let us not take each other for granted.

GAZING HEAVENWARD

If then you have been raised with Christ, seek the things that are above, where Christ is, seated at the right hand of God.

COLOSSIANS 3:1 ESV

When Christ died, we were buried with him and permanently severed from sin. When Christ rose from the dead, we were also raised out of darkness and into newness of life. Because we trust in the Lord as our Savior and accept his gift of salvation, we are forever united with him, and a seat is reserved for us in his kingdom.

It's no wonder we are exhorted to seek the things above, where Christ is, rather than the earth which is a temporary dwelling. Our time on earth is not in vain; it's intentional and important. But it is not our ultimate goal, and it should never distract us from our real, eternal identity in Christ and his kingdom.

Lord Jesus, the focus of our lives and our marriage is you. We keep our eyes on you and refuse to entertain distractions from our purpose and true identity. Please walk with us as we make decisions. Help us focus on what matters.

INCOMPATIBLE

All that is in the world—the lust of the flesh, the lust of the eyes,
and the pride of life—is not of the Father but is of the world.
And the world is passing away, and the lust of it;
but he who does the will of God abides forever.

1 JOHN 2:16-17 NKJV

Worldly goals, ideologies, philosophies, and cravings are conceived in sin and exclude heavenly objectives, principles, practices, and attitudes. In a word, the ways of the world are incompatible with God's way.

We can't profess to be children of the Father of Light if we occupy the darkness and live like the world. Our allegiance is to God's kingdom and not the world's system. Since the world operates differently from us, it is difficult at times, but God has given us everything we need to lead lives of holiness and truth. Let us live for the eternal glory of God rather than the fleeting pleasures of the world.

We'll keep our eyes and hearts on you, Jesus. Help us renounce the things of this world so we do not become enticed by lustful leanings and ungodly gratifications. In your name, we ask this.

MERCY AND BLESSINGS

*"God blesses those who are merciful,
for they will be shown mercy."*
MATTHEW 5:7 NLT

Does your spouse need more mercy in their life? Maybe they beat themselves up for not being able to accomplish more in a day, or perhaps they compare themselves to others. Maybe they don't feel fully accepted by you, God, others, or themselves.

If any of these are the case, pray about how you can practically show them more mercy today. Everyone needs more mercy and grace. Since God has abundantly lavished his mercy on us, we have enough to extend to others as well. Starting with your spouse and moving on to your other relationships, how can you exhibit more mercy and grace to those who need it?

Gracious God, the mercy and blessings we receive from you are all the inspiration we need to show others mercy as well. Thank you for helping us become more like you.

Toying with Temptation

*"Lead us not into temptation,
but deliver us from the evil one."*

Matthew 6:13 NIV

The Lord does not tempt us, but there is an enemy at work. There are times when God might test us, but that is to encourage us to do something good, not entice us to do something wrong. God does not play games with us like that because he knows how destructive sin is.

We should not play games with sin and temptation or even walk down that path. There are times to rise up and fight, and there are times to run back to the safe, loving arms of our Father God. We need his deliverance and guidance because we are not strong enough to withstand sin alone. Pray for his protection today. Do whatever you need to do to avoid sin; do not toy with it. Ask your spouse or your friends to hold you accountable and keep your eyes on Christ.

Oh Lord, you are kind, good, and honest. Temptation is from the evil one and not from you. Don't let us be fooled into thinking we can walk near temptation and be strong enough on our own to withstand it. We need you, God! Please deliver us.

WHAT IS GOOD

He has told you, O man, what is good;
*and what does the L*ORD *require of you*
but to do justice, and to love kindness,
and to walk humbly with your God?

MICAH 6:8 ESV

We complicate our theology all too often. We debate little details, the secondary points of salvation, and small bits of knowledge with little eternal significance. God, however, judges us and our conduct by a simple standard: do justice, love kindness, and walk humbly.

There is a simple standard of right and wrong, and God gave us a conscience to discern it. He also gave us hearts to act in love and kindness and spirits to be refined through humility. If we want a solid relationship with our spouse, we must base our conduct on these three things. These are what God has called good, and these are the simple things that God requires of us. The difficulty is not in understanding God's commandments but in following them.

Lord, give us the strength to walk in the refining of our hearts. Give us the strength to be committed both to your commandments and to each other. We so often fail, Lord. Remind us of your mercies and set us on your path again.

FLOURISHING

I am like an olive tree flourishing in the house of God;
I trust in God's unfailing love for ever and ever.

PSALM 52:8 NIV

Something that flourishes is not just doing well; it's doing extremely well. It's wonderful to have a flourishing marriage. There isn't a silver bullet to having a flourishing marriage, but one of the best paths to ensure it is to put God at the center. God's unfailing love will forever be the answer to a successful marriage.

Psalm 52:8 speaks of an olive tree flourishing in the house of God. Being planted and rooted in God and his Word taps directly into the heart of the marriage, and it will naturally flourish as a result. Trust in God and deepen your relationship in him for your life and your marriage to flourish.

Lord, we look to you for the source of a healthy marriage as we live out your Word in faith. We commit to each other and to you. We want every word and behavior to reflect your love. May we treat each other well so our marriage is like a tree planted by water to flourish.

GOD'S COMMANDMENTS

This is the love of God, that we keep his commandments.
And his commandments are not burdensome.
1 JOHN 5:3 ESV

Is it difficult to recognize that God's love and commandments are intricately intertwined? That is what this passage tells us. To show the love of God, we must keep his commandments. God's commandments are more than a set of dos and don'ts, and their purpose is not simply to lead us to repentance; they teach us how to love. His commandments mold us into people who love like Jesus loves.

A reckless, lawless person is not in the condition required to show God's love to others. A humble, penitent person is one who keeps God's commandments and discovers the glorious love which accompanies them. That is why laws are not "burdensome," for we can't be weighed down by something that fills us with the love of God.

Lord, humble us beneath your loving commandments. Let them be the hands of a skilled and patient potter shaping clay. Make us into vessels of your love for those around us and for the person closest to our hearts.

TRUE VALUABLES

"Sell your possessions and give to the poor. Provide purses for yourselves that will not wear out, a treasure in heaven that will never fail, where no thief comes near and no moth destroys. For where your treasure is, there your heart will be also."

LUKE 12:33-34 NIV

God wants us to be good stewards of the resources he puts in our hands. The land around us, the wealth we accumulate, and the possessions we have are all actually God's, and he wants us to use them as good kingdom citizens. Yet in the midst of this prudent stewardship, he also wants us to be reckless in our generosity. He wants us to know that no matter the amount of money in our retirement account, it is ultimately fleeting and worthless. He wants us to live in the knowledge of true valuables.

Generosity, compassion, love, and commitment are investments that will last into eternity. When we value the things of God, we find that our hearts belong to God. We find that by putting our hearts toward the things that matter to God, we become more like him. Our marriages will not last forever. This can make our love feel fruitless, but the fruit of marriage still exists. It exists in the virtue we cultivate with our spouses by living a communal life.

God, make us people who value what you value so we may grow into your image.

Purpose in Marriage

Has not the one God made you? You belong to him in body and spirit. And what does the one God seek? Godly offspring. So be on your guard, and do not be unfaithful to the wife of your youth.

MALACHI 2:15 NIV

As we navigate the chaos of our world, we witness many marriages devoid of happiness, joy, or peace. That special love shared between partners has faded. Marriages founded on the principles of God's Word, by people who find their fulfillment in the Lord, tend to bear more fruit and be more content.

Couples who have the Lord as their guide and comforter don't expect their spouse to satisfy all their needs because they know no human is capable of that. The children of this couple have a strong foundation. The ministry of this couple has purpose and direction. The union between this couple is more loving and realistic. Their guard is up, their fruit is plentiful, and their relationship with the Lord is blessed.

Dear Lord, we pray for peace, love, and understanding between us. Our desire for our marriage is that it honors you in all we do.

POWER OF UNITY

Two people are better off than one,
for they can help each other succeed.
ECCLESIASTES 4:9 NLT

Have you ever realized how much faster and better you work when you're working with someone you trust? Besides, it's more fun than working alone. When a problem arises and you're working alone, it can quickly become overwhelming and discouraging. Burdens lighten when someone else helps you carry them.

God knew this when he instigated marriage. What an incredible gift to have someone by your side to walk life's highs and lows with you! Unity within marriage makes life richer and more fulfilling than a marriage simply comprised of two individuals living their own lives. Let's learn to walk together, lean on each other, and embrace the ups and downs together.

Your design is so great, dear God, and we're thrilled to be part of it! Thank you for bringing us together. May we celebrate good times together, help each other through hard times, and always stand together to praise and worship you.

WATCHING OVER US

He stores up sound wisdom for the upright;
He is a shield to those who walk in integrity,
Guarding the paths of justice,
And He watches over the way of His godly ones.
PROVERBS 2:7-8 NASB

It feels good to know that someone is looking out for us. That includes looking out for our well-being and for everything that concerns us including our marriages. Friends, parents, pastors, and others can lift our spirits with their support, but no one can be there in every moment.

Sometimes life feels overwhelming, but we are never left alone. God himself is our shield and strength. He gives us the wisdom we require and keeps us on the right path. Let's walk with confidence and integrity knowing we are protected on all sides.

Lord, we know that unless you watch over a city, the builders build in vain. Unless you watch over our marriage, all our efforts are in vain as well. Thank you, therefore, for watching over us.

EVERLASTING IMPACT

We fix our eyes not on what is seen, but on what is unseen,
since what is seen is temporary, but what is unseen is eternal.
2 CORINTHIANS 4:18 NIV

The Bible tells us to focus on what is unseen rather than what is seen. It tells us to focus on our faith, our marriage, our relationship with God, and other things that are not temporary but have an everlasting impact. God wants us to focus on what matters most in life and what will bring us the most joy and fulfillment, and that is our relationship with him, our spouses and families, and the broader Christian community.

When we look back on our lives, these are the things that will count rather than the physical, tangible things we see. Our God loves relationships and places high value on them, and he wants us to do the same. What unseen, eternal gift is going unnoticed in your life today?

Eternal God, give us eyes to see what is everlasting and the wisdom to focus our energy on these things. Our relationship with you matters more than anything to us.

INSEPARABLE

I am persuaded that neither death nor life, nor angels nor principalities nor powers, nor things present nor things to come, nor height nor depth, nor any other created thing, shall be able to separate us from the love of God which is in Christ Jesus our Lord.
ROMANS 8:38-39 NKJV

During their wedding vows, almost every couple promises to love and cherish each other until death parts them. Our romantic relationships on earth are not eternal, and we can't count on them as something that has always been and always will be. That is the place for God's love. "Neither death, nor life," Paul says. The final end of every human's earthly existence, as well as the bountiful force of existence itself, have no power over the love God has for us.

How incredible it is to be loved while unworthy! We could never earn an iota of God's favor, yet he chooses to bestow heaping measures on us. How can we be ungrateful in light of our inseparable bond to our Savior and in light of his love for us? No, the trials on earth are nothing compared to this glory. There is not "any created thing" comparable to the love of God which triumphs over all.

Dear Savior, how wonderful is your love for us. Despite all the losses and changes of life, we are inseparable from your abundant love. Thank you, Lord, for giving your Son for this.

LOVING THE VISIBLE

If someone says, "I love God," and yet he hates his brother or sister,
he is a liar; for the one who does not love his brother and sister
whom he has seen, cannot love God, whom he has not seen.

1 JOHN 4:20 NASB

It's easy to live in our heads. It's simple to love the idea of a spouse as the airbrushed version of whom we imagined we would one day marry. Once we are bound to someone in matrimony, however, we have committed ourselves to the earthly, the imperfect, and the rough-edged. Sometimes, partners act unlovable, yet we are still able to love because of the love of God working in us. In those moments, we can show God how much we love him by loving them.

Next time you see your spouse's earthly imperfection—their real, raw humanity—choose to love them through it. If we hate the visible people around us, then we cannot love the invisible God. We put his love into practice through our love of the people around us. Devotion to a real, regular person, not the ideal we construct in our head, is what genuine, heartfelt commitment looks like.

Dear Lord, thank you for loving us in our mortality. Thank you for choosing to redeem an earthly, mortal race. Please give us the courage to love others the same way.

WEIGHTY MATTERS

A man who makes a vow to the LORD or makes a pledge under oath must never break it. He must do exactly what he said he would do.
NUMBERS 30:2 NLT

In today's world, unfortunately, marriage has been trivialized, and even believers can lose sight of the value God has placed on marriage as it says in Numbers 30:2. Even though marriage is under assault in the world, we know that the coming together of two people in honor to God is a union that has profound consequences both now in our earthly lives as well as in the spiritual realm.

Marriage needs to be respected by all parties, and we should always have the intention of honoring the vows we spoke to each other before God and witnesses. Words matter, and the words spoken in our marriage vows are particularly important.

Lord, you are the author of marriage, and we want to honor the vows of our marriage before you and men. Help us be faithful and honor you in our marriage. May we bring glory to you through our marriage union in everything we do, say, and think. Thank you for giving us a blueprint on how to honor you in the institution of marriage.

Favor with God

"Who then is a faithful and wise servant, whom his master made ruler over his household, to give them food in due season? Blessed is that servant whom his master, when he comes, will find so doing. Assuredly, I say to you that he will make him ruler over all his goods."

MATTHEW 24:45-47 NKJV

Marriage is a ministry. If you understand that, your whole outlook on marriage changes in a massive way. As believers, we understand that the first opportunity for ministry is in our own households. Your position as a husband or wife is an engagement from God and is a service to him. You can't neglect your marriage and then claim to be doing ministry elsewhere.

The health of your marriage reflects your walk with God and a statement about the importance you put on God's presence in your life. According to today's verses from Matthew, God is watching how we carry out our marriage and the life he has given us. When we show our willingness to follow his plan and purpose, he will expand our responsibilities.

Lord, every good gift comes from you, and we thank you. You ask us to be faithful with what you have entrusted to us including our spouse and our marriage. May we honor you and each other in the life you have called us to.

BE KIND

Be kind to one another, compassionate, forgiving each other,
just as God in Christ also has forgiven you.
EPHESIANS 4:32 NASB

Do you truly understand God's saving grace? Does it motivate you to live a godly life? It can be the greatest motivation! When we come to grips with all we have been forgiven of and saved from, we change. We yearn to live in a way that honors this gift. As Christians, we do not do good things to earn our salvation; we do good things because of our immense gratitude for our salvation.

Christians are part of a single, unified family: the body of Christ. Within that body, we are assigned different talents and tasks. For the body of believers to work well together for the glory of God, we need to be kind and compassionate. We need to be forgiving. When that's difficult, we can remember we have been forgiven too. This is important within marriage. How can a marriage operate for the glory of God if it's lacking kindness, compassion, or forgiveness? It can't.

Father, thank you for the roles we have within your body of believers. We also thank you for our roles in this relationship. For your glory, we want to make kindness, compassion, and forgiveness foundational merits of our marriage.

LOVE AND SUBMISSION

Wives, be subject to your husbands, as is fitting in the Lord.
Husbands, love your wives and do not become bitter against them.
COLOSSIANS 3:18-19 NASB

God is always calling us to higher maturity. Marriage is designed to bless us and also push us to a spiritually deeper way of living. The Bible instructs wives to cooperate in helping their husbands. They have been given the opportunity and commission to aid them because Christ aided us. Husbands have an emotional obligation to their wives. God expects them to demonstrate sacrificial love and caring patience for them because that is how God acts toward us. This doesn't mean wives shouldn't have patience and love or husbands shouldn't help their wives, but it does mean each has a specific calling that reflects God.

Whenever we struggle in our calling, we have Christ to look at as an example. His glorious submission and love were neither required nor deserved, yet he gave both freely. That is how we ought to be in our service to each other too.

Holy Jesus, may our marriage be driven by love and sacrifice and never by self-interest. Thank you for giving us a real, up-close, perfect example of what a life of love and service looks like.

AUTHORITY

Remind the people to be subject to rulers and authorities, to be obedient, to be ready to do whatever is good, to slander no one, to be peaceable and considerate, and always to be gentle toward everyone.
TITUS 3:1-2 NIV

Do you speak disrespectfully about the president, your pastor, or your boss? What words to you say behind closed doors when it is only you and your spouse? Even there, what we say matters because it reveals the condition of our heart.

We may disagree with things our leaders say or do, but there is a way to discuss them without slander. They are under God too, and they will answer to him in the end. Rather than let evil speech seep out of our mouths where peace and praise ought to be, let us guard our words and trust God to judge those in authority.

It is you who establishes authority, Father God. When we disagree with our leaders, help us do so respectfully. We want to be ready to do whatever is good.

PURPOSEFUL SUFFERING

Let those who suffer according to the will of God commit their souls to Him in doing good, as to a faithful Creator.

1 PETER 4:19 NKJV

How should Christians respond to suffering in this life and especially to the suffering caused by being associated with Jesus? First, let's remember that suffering isn't necessarily bad. We're taught to desire what is easy and painless, but some lessons can only be learned through suffering. What's more, our unshakable hope in the face of suffering is a powerful testimony of the peace of God. This kind of testimony can't be explained; it can only be experienced.

Understanding that we will experience difficult times as part of God's plan can help us maintain proper perspective. Refusal to succumb to hopelessness is a declaration to God, ourselves, and the world around us that we will not wait for circumstances to improve before we call God good. We believe that our good God is there with us, caring for us through our suffering, just as he always does.

Faithful Creator, we commit our souls to you. Whether we have good days or difficult days, good years or difficult years, we submit to your better plan. We don't know how it will unfold, but if you are guiding us, we are heading in the best direction.

WATCH YOUR WORDS

If anyone thinks he is religious and does not bridle his tongue but deceives his heart, this person's religion is worthless.
JAMES 1:26 ESV

Words can build, and words can destroy. We need to be extremely careful about what words we put in the air. This is especially true within marriage. What we say and how we say it reflects what is inside our hearts. Our speech betrays our spiritual condition. Fresh water does not produce a salty spring any more than salty water produces a fresh spring (James 3:11), and our hearts and mouths are no different. Our words are a good gauge for where our hearts truly lie.

Perhaps you think you're doing well because you're adhering to religious niceties, but have you been getting angry easily? Are you complaining a lot? Do you gossip about other people or slander them? Are you always pointing out the negative first? Pay close attention because you may be deceiving yourself. What good is your testimony to others if your words are not encouraging? Can you be a blessing to your spouse if your speech is always negative?

Please help us, dear Father, to address the issues in our hearts so our words are wise and helpful rather than bitter and hurtful. We want to be a blessing to each other and a testimony to your goodness.

BE TRUTHFUL

Putting away lying, "Let each one of you speak truth with his neighbor," for we are members of one another.
EPHESIANS 4:25 NKJV

Trust is hard to earn and easy to lose. As members of the body of Christ, we strive to an even higher level of honest living and genuine speech because we represent the personhood of truth himself. A marriage cannot thrive when intermingled with dishonesty, and a ministry cannot be fruitful by displaying a fictitious form of godliness.

The person who puts away all falsehood and speaks the truth in love, trusting God and doing the right thing no matter the consequences, will undoubtedly experience growth and blessing in their marriage, their job, their community relationships, and their life as a whole. This is how we are to act as members of the same body and as one in Christ.

Heavenly Father, examine our hearts and expose any areas displeasing to you. Root out hypocrisy from our lives and remove any mask of pretense we may hide behind. We want to speak the truth and live in the light.

LOYAL FRIENDS

A friend loves at all times,
and a brother is born for a time of adversity.
PROVERBS 17:17 NIV

Beyond your marriage partnership, do you and your spouse share a friendship? What key features of your union display the level of love and intimacy and joy that God wants for you to experience together? Hard times can bond people the most and reveal who their real friends are. Fairweather friends will flee when times get tough, but a true friend will loyally stick with you in your time of need.

If you and your spouse have seen tough times together, perhaps they worked to strengthen your marriage and your friendship. When you choose to loyally stick together and serve God side by side through good and hard times, a deep friendship is bound to bloom.

Lord, thank you for this marriage and the friendship we share. Thank you for the good days we have shared and the hard days which strengthened us and taught us loyalty. May we continue to grow closer to each other and to you.

IMITATE GOD

Imitate God, therefore, in everything you do,
because you are his dear children.
EPHESIANS 5:1 NLT

Children learn from the influence of their parents. They begin imitating them as soon as they learn to talk, and they keep imitating them, either consciously or subconsciously, for the rest of their lives.

If we are God's children, we will follow God's example. That means not taking part in actions, attitudes, and motives unacceptable to God. It means walking in the Spirit by sharing the truth in love, growing in grace, and learning obedience through suffering. It entails putting away the influences and characteristics of our old sinful natures and their wide range of outward actions, inward attitudes, and secret motives which are unacceptable in children of God. We are dear to God, and he cares about our growth. He has given us everything we need to live in truth and righteousness.

Loving Father, we want to be more and more like Christ, to walk in newness of life, and to truly reflect you to the world. Thank you for your example and influence.

WATCH

*Watch, stand fast in the faith,
be brave, be strong.*
1 CORINTHIANS 16:13 NKJV

Doesn't life seem like a series of challenges? Once you conquer one, another one is already waiting for you. It is discouraging at times, but just remember that we already have the victory and are more than conquerors in all things (Rom. 8:37). Rather than giving way to anxiety or defeat, let's be brave and strong, immovable in our faith, and witness what God does through us.

With Christ, we can face our troubles head-on. How can we respond practically to challenges within marriage? What does it look like to stand fast in our faith when it comes to how we love and live with a spouse?

Lord, some days are hard, but we thank you for the victory which is already ours through you. We never need to be overwhelmed because you have us in your hands.

April

Love flashes like fire,

the brightest kind of flame.

Many waters cannot quench love,

nor can rivers drown it.

Song of Solomon 8:6-7 NLT

INTEGRITY AND DEVOTION

I devoted myself to the work on this wall.
All my men were assembled there for the work;
we did not acquire any land.

NEHEMIAH 5:16 NIV

When was the last time God gave you a task that demanded your full attention? Have you ever been called to a work greater than your own personal interests? Nehemiah was so committed to working on Jerusalem's wall that he gave it his constant attention. While building the wall, Nehemiah kept his integrity by not purchasing any of the land from poverty-stricken locals. Even though he could have acquired it for far less than it was worth, he refused to take advantage of their plight.

Perhaps your marriage is in a good season or a difficult one; regardless, it is a work worthy of constant attention and upkeep. Like Nehemiah, we must maintain our morals and integrity and never take advantage of those going through a tough time. If your spouse is struggling, don't belittle them or exploit their situation. Instead, come alongside them and stay committed to the work of the Lord. Stay committed to your marriage.

Father God, thank you for the example of commitment and unwavering devotion you left us through your servant Nehemiah. May we be a shining example of loyalty to what you have called us to as well.

GOD'S FAITHFULNESS

Know therefore that the LORD your God is God; he is the faithful
God, keeping his covenant of love to a thousand generations
of those who love him and keep his commandments.

DEUTERONOMY 7:9 NIV

Many of us have insurance on our houses, our cars, or our health. The main purpose of insurance is to confirm that help will be there on a rainy day when we need it most. God also works to hedge against a rainy day, but he does so much more. In today's very, we read that God is faithful to keep his promises.

In marriage, you need to be faithful and dependable for your spouse who, hopefully, returns the same. If you and your spouse can count on each other when things get tough, then God's plan has the foundation to grow. His Word is faithful if we remain in him and keep his commandments, and this includes our marriages. God will uphold and sustain our marriages if we keep God at the center.

Lord, thank you for your faithfulness in our walk with you and in our marriage. We are in awe of your faithfulness. We are forever grateful for this assurance in you and in your Word. We want to dive deeper and discover more about you.

BELIEVE AND TURN

The Lord's hand was with them,
and a great number of people believed and turned to the Lord.
ACTS 11:21 NIV

The progression of events laid out in this verse is, in a nutshell, the gospel message. First, God reaches out his hand to us and gives us faith. Second, we believe what he says is true. Finally, we accept his hand by turning away from the world and turning to him. When the Lord reached out to the Gentiles and so many of them believed and turned, the gospel message spread like wildfire.

There is nothing more powerful than a touch from God and nothing more contagious than a changed sinner. A touch from God does not mean our lives will be perfect and we'll never slip into sin again, but it isn't possible to be touched by God and not be changed. When we believe him and turn to him, the changes will be obvious to us and everyone around us.

Lord, continue to be with us and touch us the same way you did when you first reached out. You have changed our lives forever. May we daily remember to turn from the world and back to you. We know your hand is with us wherever we go.

Prayer Is Central

Continue earnestly in prayer,
being vigilant in it with thanksgiving.
Colossians 4:2 NKJV

Through prayer, we admit our dependence on our heavenly Father. Through prayer, we call for him to work in our lives. Through prayer, we express a living trust that he will answer our cries and fulfill our needs according to his will. Without prayer as a focal part of our day, in our marriage, and in all other relationships, we flaunt independence from him and demonstrate a self-sufficient attitude that dishonors his name and invites trouble and temptation.

We are not wise enough to guard ourselves on all sides, but God is, and he's happy to do so. Let's be vigilant in our prayer life and remember all the things we can thank God for. That will keep our hearts focused and keep the ways of the flesh at bay.

It is amazing to us, Lord, that we don't need any special exemptions or clearance to come and talk to you. You are King of the universe, and yet you are also our Father. We realize how important it is to connect with you regularly, so we will pray in reverence to you as our powerful King and in adoration as our loving Father.

TRUSTWORTHY

I want you to understand that the head of every man is Christ,
the head of a wife is her husband, and the head of Christ is God.
1 CORINTHIANS 11:3 ESV

The ways of God are far above our ways. We don't always understand, but we know that God is trustworthy and our ultimate authority. Within marriage, it is vital that we be trustworthy too. Depending on the setting, a spouse might need to represent both parties or make decisions on their partner's behalf. There needs to be trust within a marriage. God led Christ, and Christ came to earth to lead us by example.

Husbands have been placed in a unique role to lead their families and are expected to do so with the kind of love and care Christ shows us. Each of us have important roles to play, and God made it so we would need each other. Let's support each other the best we can, submit to God's authority, and strive to be as trustworthy as possible for the sake of our beloved spouse.

Lord, thank you for your authority and leadership. Without you, there is chaos. You bring order and peace, and your faithfulness makes trusting you an easy decision. Teach us to trust each other, submit to each other, and be trustworthy ourselves.

OUR COMFORTER

Let your steadfast love comfort me
according to your promise to your servant.
PSALM 119:76 ESV

In this Scripture, the Lord made us a promise to be there for us and offer us comfort. There are days when we may feel completely defeated, almost like we're drowning, as difficult situations challenge our sense of comfort and security in God. Maybe your marriage feels more like a curse than a blessing. Maybe your job feels like a cage instead of an opportunity.

On such days, we can rely on God's promise of love and comfort and know the Holy Spirit is there whether we feel him or not. When we do feel him, it can breathe new life into our marriage, jobs, ministry, or whatever else we need encouragement for. On such days, soak in that refreshing comfort that offers direction and purpose. Problems come and go, but God's love and comfort is constant.

We seek our asylum in you, Holy Spirit. You are our comfort and the lover of our souls. Thank you for being there to help us in the difficult days and share in the good times. We love you.

RUNNING TO HEAVEN

Brothers and sisters, I do not regard myself as having taken hold of it yet; but one thing I do: forgetting what lies behind and reaching forward to what lies ahead, I press on toward the goal for the prize of the upward call of God in Christ Jesus.

PHILIPPIANS 3:13-14 NASB

Do you have a past that haunts you? Are there sins in your past which still tempt you? Not one of us is perfect; not a single one of us has "taken hold of it yet," but we press on. We look forward and not backward. It's important to forgive ourselves of our past mistakes just as Christ has already forgiven us.

When temptation looms, let's keep our eyes on the prize and remember how immeasurably more gratifying it is and worthy of our time. Our new goal is to run forward into the calling God has placed on each of us, and he's here to help us every step of the way.

Dear Father, as we walk this marriage path together, lead us and keep our eyes focused on you instead of on the regrets of our past. Help us be there for each other as a strength and encouragement to move forward.

RUTH'S DEVOTION

"Do not urge me to leave you or to return from following you.
For where you go I will go, and where you lodge I will lodge.
Your people shall be my people, and your God my God.
Where you die I will die, and there will I be buried.
May the Lord do so to me and more also if anything
but death parts me from you."

RUTH 1:16-17 ESV

One of the most compelling stories in the Bible about commitment, love, and honor is the story of Ruth. As a young, newly widowed woman who had other options, she could have taken an easier path rather than follow her destitute mother-in-law back to her homeland, but Ruth loved Naomi. God saw her faithfulness, took care of her, and even included her, a foreigner, in the lineage of Jesus.

Ruth is a powerful example of how God works in our lives when we stick to what we know is right and loving even when times are tough. In the end, God's way is the best way, and the more difficult path of love is always worthwhile.

Father God, please grow in us the perseverance and commitment Ruth had. We want our love to remain the same through thick and thin.

CAPTIVATED

Let your wife be a fountain of blessing for you.
Rejoice in the wife of your youth.
She is a loving deer, a graceful doe.
Let her breasts satisfy you always.
May you always be captivated by her love.

PROVERBS 5:18-19 NLT

In his writing, Solomon advises his students to take joy in their relationship, and a key part of that joy is sexually. Marriage offers a unique sense of care and intimacy. It was designed by God to connect two people together emotionally, physically, and spiritually.

Husbands and wives should pursue each other and find ways to bless one another throughout the duration of their marriage. "Rejoice in the wife of your youth" is both an encouragement and a caution. If you have been married for many years, don't forget the love you have shared with your spouse. It is irreplaceable, and you can't replicate it with someone else. Remain captivated by each other. A marriage like this is beautiful and rare.

Almighty God and Creator, your design of marriage is profound and wonderful. It offers such a vivid example of how Christ loves us. Please continue to teach us how to love each other like you love us.

Meditate on the Word

Keep this Book of the Law always on your lips;
meditate on it day and night, so that you may be careful to do
everything written in it. Then you will be prosperous and successful.

Joshua 1:8 niv

What we surround ourselves with influences us. The people we hang out with, the music we listen to, what we watch on television: they impact how we think, feel, and reason. We are what we eat, or rather, what we consume. When we're immersed in the Word of God, reading it, studying it, listening to it, and memorizing it, we soak in its wisdom and learn to walk in God's ways. That is the only way to be prosperous and successful in what truly matters.

Do you want your marriage to be prosperous? Scripture should play a big role. Do you want your life to be a success? Apply the Bible to it.

Day and night, Lord, we will surround ourselves with good influences instead of destructive ones. We will read your Word, learn from it, and apply it to our lives. Your Word brings us life.

SOFT HEARTS

"I will give them one heart, and put a new spirit within them.
And I will remove the heart of stone from their flesh
and give them a heart of flesh."

EZEKIEL 11:19 NASB

Even if you don't agree with your spouse on everything socially, theologically, or politically, if you share a common love for the Lord, that is a strong connector. Christians may debate the small stuff, but in the end, we should all be able to come together under the cross of Christ.

It is a dangerous path to get legalistically caught up in the details of life, love, and the Scriptures. Our hearts grow cold, and we refuse to consider others' perspectives. Even then, God is willing to soften our hard hearts and put his Spirit in us. Soft hearts hurt for the hurting and hear the cries of the broken. Soft hearts are more easily unified, and they love deeply. You need two soft hearts to experience an incredible marriage, so ask God to soften yours today. Don't let petty issues or minor differences harden your heart.

Heavenly Father, we ask that you soften our hearts again. Please help us shake off offense, embrace our differences, and not get caught up in disagreements. We want one heart together with you, each other, and our Christian brothers and sisters.

CLEAN

If we confess our sins, he is faithful and just to forgive us our sins and to cleanse us from all unrighteousness.

1 JOHN 1:9 ESV

The overarching story between God and humanity is God's forgiveness of human sin and the restoration of the relationship between God and his people through the death and resurrection of Jesus. The Bible says Christ had to die for us so we could be reconciled to God. For this reason, we are expected to forgive as we have been forgiven.

In the context of marriage, that divine grace extended to us will be needed one way or another. Your spouse may wrong you, but you also will do wrong at some point and need grace. Extend forgiveness toward your guilty spouse. There is no perfect marriage, only a perfect God, and every person is imperfect and dependent upon him. Today let us remember to have forgiving hearts and graceful attitudes toward our spouses. Forgiveness is important for a healthy and flourishing marriage. It honors God, and it is in obedience to his Word.

Lord, thank for the forgiveness you have shown us. While we were still sinners, you died for us. Let us have the same attitude in our marriage as you have toward us. Help us grow in grace and be quick to forgive. May we not hold grudges toward each other.

Hand in Hand

Though he fall, he shall not be cast headlong,
for the Lord upholds his hand.
PSALM 37:24 ESV

We cannot make a mistake so terrible that the Lord would not catch us. There are sins so offensive that we, as humans, struggle to forgive each other, but the Lord's forgiveness is always available to anyone who asks with a contrite heart.

When our spouses hurt us, it may be difficult to pardon them and not hold a grudge, but it is possible because of the great love and forgiveness we have been shown. How can we hold a debt against someone when our great debt was wiped out completely? Our spouses will disappoint us at times, and we're going to let them down too. But we can learn from the Lord to hold their hands, forgive them, and help keep them from falling.

You never leave us alone, dear God. You hold our hands and keep us from falling. As we stumble along and make mistakes, we lean on your grace, and we will extend grace to each other as well.

RACE TO WIN

Do you not know that in a race all the runners run,
but only one gets the prize?
Run in such a way as to get the prize.
1 CORINTHIANS 9:24 NIV

If we hobble along half-heartedly in this race of life, we aren't running for a prize; we're simply running to make it to the end. We can enjoy the consolation of salvation, but God has so much more to give us. He has things he wants to show us, but we need to look. He has things he wants to tell us when we're ready to listen.

Are you running or are you racing? Are you running around in life, distracted and busy, doing a lot of work but getting nothing done? Or are you racing with your eyes on the prize of Christ Jesus? Is your life focused and are your efforts intentional? Keep your eyes on Jesus, and you'll never miss a step. You will run like a formidable athlete, determined to win.

We're running, Lord, but we want it to matter.
Show us which way to go so we can race to win.

On Our Side

"The LORD your God in your midst,
The Mighty One, will save;
He will rejoice over you with gladness,
He will quiet you with His love,
He will rejoice over you with singing."

ZEPHANIAH 3:17 NKJV

Imagine a school playground at recess. The class bully is out to make mischief, and he carefully ponders who today's victim will be. He notices one small, frail boy playing by himself, but he quickly dismisses that option. He is untouchable. Why? Because that weak, young boy has an older brother, and the bully knows better than to pick a fight with him.

Similarly, God watches over us. The devil may try to mess with us, but when we invoke the name of our loving Lord and Savior, he runs and hides. Our bully knows which lines he cannot cross with us too.

Thank you for always protecting us, dear Father. Even when we don't realize it, you're keeping our enemy at bay.

Relationships Matter

*"Where two or three are gathered in my name,
there am I among them."*
Matthew 18:20 esv

God loves relationships; that can't be overstated. He has so much love to give that he created us, and he created us to love each other. All the love we feel is an outpouring of his love which he put in us. The love felt between parent-child relationships, spouses, and friends are all different pictures of God's love for us. He calls us his children, his bride, and his friends.

When we are with each other, sharing heavy burdens or spending causal time, God delights in the fact that his children are enjoying each other's company. When we spend quality time with our spouses, loving them and caring for them, he is overjoyed that we are delighting in the partners he entrusted to us. God wants us to spend time with him, and he wants us to spend time with each other.

We truly delight in you, God, and we delight in each other. Thank you for filling our lives with meaningful relationships.

STAYING THE COURSE

I have fought the good fight,
I have finished the race,
I have kept the faith.
2 TIMOTHY 4:7 NKJV

Consider the roles God has assigned you. Are you a husband or wife? A parent or grandparent? An employee or boss? A missionary or pastor? What work have you been assigned as an image-bearer of Christ? How has God designed you to fit as a member of his body and your local church? What role do you play in the making and maturing of disciples of Jesus?

Frankly, you could be a CEO or a grocery bagger, childless or a parent of ten children, but what matters is carrying out your God-given role faithfully. Faith is not a sprint, and neither is marriage, ministry, or any lasting area of life. We are called to be faithful to the end so that, like Paul, we can say we have fought the fight, stayed faithful, and finished the work God gave us to do.

Whatever you have given us to do, Lord Jesus, we want to do it faithfully. Thank you for giving us each other to walk as partners through this life with you.

God's Preparations

"No eye has seen, no ear has heard, and no mind has imagined what God has prepared for those who love him."

1 Corinthians 2:9 NLT

Your future is less uncertain than you might think. Perhaps you're stuck in a dead-end job, floating between houses, or pushing through the daily grind with no end in sight. Whatever the case, your path is not random or hopeless. God has plans for how he wants to use his loved ones who rely on him and are ready to follow his lead.

We can't know what "no eye has seen, no ear has heard, and no mind has imagined," but it is possible for us to know God. When we think about the future, our minds constantly play out different scenarios and possibilities, but God's plans are better than we can imagine. He has glorious plans for our time on earth; even more glorious are the plans for when we rise again with him! Then we will be able to see the greatest of God's preparations: the home he has prepared for us.

Lord in heaven, give us faith in the plans you have in mind. We want to dedicate ourselves to your plans, not our own, no matter how unpredictable they seem. Give us faith in your preparations.

HOSPITALITY

Let brotherly love continue. Do not forget to entertain strangers,
for by so doing some have unwittingly entertained angels.
HEBREWS 13:1-2 NKJV

Not all love is romantic. Different kinds of love are similar in their quality of selflessness, self-effacement, devotion, and emotional investment. The brotherly love in this passage aims at being hospitable and welcoming to those who might not have anything to give back. When we only pour love into the people who are most important to us, we might discover it's not love at all. It might just be love for the sake of our emotional safety and satisfaction.

To nurture the love we have for our spouses, we have to love all the people in our lives, even those we cross paths with randomly. This is what Lot did with the angels at his doorstep, and it secured him the favor of God and safety from destruction. We are wise to wear the love of God proudly on our sleeves. Love should not be hidden and taken out only for those closest to us; it must be poured out like an aroma that surrounds us.

God, give us a spirit of brotherly love and hospitality. Make us people who bring in the cold and broken, help the needy, and reach out for your name's sake.

Righteous Bodies

Do not let any part of your body become an instrument of evil to serve sin. Instead, give yourselves completely to God, for you were dead, but now you have new life. So use your whole body as an instrument to do what is right for the glory of God.

Romans 6:13 NLT

An instrument is anything that can be used. In the context of this verse, the individual parts of our bodies can be defined as instruments of righteousness or evil depending on how we use them. According to the Bible, our bodies do not belong to us but to our spouses (1 Cor. 7:4). If we use the members of our body to seek sexual satisfaction apart from our partners, it is an unrighteous act. It is a symptom of spiritual weakness that often stems from a misunderstanding of God's design or a lack of self-control.

In Christ, we have the understanding we need to commit our bodies to acts of righteousness. This commitment is first and foremost to God and respects his original design. This commitment is also to our spouses as we dedicate our bodies to their ownership rather than our own.

Almighty Savior, give us strength to remain pure and righteous. Make our bodies instruments of your purpose to fulfill your design and desires rather than our own. We dedicate our bodies and their instruments to you and to each other.

Stay Clean

You were bought at a price;
therefore glorify God in your body and in your spirit,
which are God's.

1 Corinthians 6:20 NKJV

When we keep our bodies holy and undistracted by sin, it is a beautiful act of gratitude and service to God. Jesus paid an incredibly high price for us to walk in freedom, so why would we clasp on chains again? Why play games with the one who wants to enslave and kill us? God has a glorious plan in mind for each of us, and he asks that we trust him. We don't know how amazing it will be until we say no to ourselves, yes to him, and walk his way for a while.

In God's plan, marriage has no room in it for other sexual participants. God created sex to be shared within marriage, and there are so many reasons why this is the best, safest, most intimate way for us to experience it. The use of our bodies is one more way we can serve God and, like everything else, we end up reaping the blessings when we submit to God's perfect design.

Thank you for saving us when we were lost in sin, glorious God. Thank you for renewing us and holding a place for us in your grand plan. We commit our bodies to you and to each other, and we refuse to dabble in sexual sin; we won't give the devil that satisfaction. Help us stay strong, committed, and pure, and please give us the courage to come back to you if we slip up.

GRACE AND MERCY

Because of his great love for us, God, who is rich in mercy,
made us alive with Christ even when we were dead in transgressions—
it is by grace you have been saved.
EPHESIANS 2:4-5 NIV

There is a clear distinction between God's grace and our deservedness. In spite of our lack of obedience, God made a way for our salvation because of his tremendous love and grace. It is only by his mercy and grace that God forgives us and not because we have earned it. In this Scripture, Paul reiterates that human effort has no impact on salvation. We were as good as dead. We had no bragging rights. Grace forgives, mercy restores, and we are the chosen recipients of both.

The next time your spouse does not deserve your grace or forgiveness, recall the way God has treated you and remember that your spouse is also his beloved child. Grace and mercy need to be present in marriage, even when it feels like an imbalance, because we have received perfect grace and mercy.

We are so grateful, dear Lord, that you showed us your grace and mercy when we were devoid of both. You have upheld us by your righteousness and saved us from the death our sins deserved. Please remind us of this whenever we are in a position to extend grace and mercy to each other. That is how we can honor your gift to us.

STAYING THE COURSE

Let us not neglect our meeting together, as some people do,
but encourage one another, especially now that
the day of his return is drawing near.
HEBREWS 10:25 NLT

During good times, complacency can set in, and we allow things to fall into disrepair and mediocrity. Marriage requires intentionality even in good times and more than in our other relationships. Hebrews 10:25 emphasizes the importance of intentionally meeting together, encouraging each other, and not neglecting one another. We should not grow complacent in doing things that are worthwhile and meaningful in our relationships.

Why not start reading the Bible or praying regularly together? It's easy to let things slide if you don't make a point of being intentional. Especially in marriage, familiarity can set in, and suddenly you don't have that purposeful time of reading and praying together. Time together opens the door to appreciating each other, and it can protect against taking your spouse for granted. Lack of time spent pursuing God together can breed resentment and frustration. Cultivate and keep a proactive attitude in marriage.

Lord, thank you for your Word and your guidance. The Scriptures say we should not give up on meeting and encouraging each other. Help us to be intentional and not slide into complacency in our marriage. Give us a spirit of excellence in all that we do.

BROKEN PROMISES

If we are faithless, He remains faithful,
for He cannot deny Himself.

2 TIMOTHY 2:13 NASB

Before God made a covenant between himself and humanity, he knew we would fail and break our promises to him, yet it did not deter him. Although we have not been faithful to hold up our end of things, God has. He keeps his promises, stays faithful to us, and will never let us down—not because we deserve it but because that is his character.

Let's remember this when our spouses let us down. Sometimes we feel the urge to even the score or drop our end of the bargain too. Who would blame us? They did it first! But that's not how the redeemed of the Lord are expected to operate. When your spouse lets you down, stay faithful. Stay constant, reliable, and loyal, and help them get back on their feet. When the tables turn and you're the one down, they will be there for you.

Almighty God, your faithfulness convicts us to brush off our failures and get back on track. Thank you for never giving up on us and holding to your promises even though we don't always hold to ours. Help us do better, dear Lord.

BENEFITS AND BURDENS

Her husband can trust her, and she will greatly enrich his life.
She brings him good, not harm, all the days of her life.
PROVERBS 31:11-12 NLT

As spouses, we should aim to build each other up in encouragement and strength. If we pull our spouses down from where they would be without us, we have become a burden to them. There are times when we will need support and be able to render little in return, but when it comes to our spiritual health, we should aim for the place where our spirit is an encouragement and safe space for our partners.

The wife of Proverbs 31 is trustworthy and "brings him good, not harm, all the days of her life." She renders support through her decisions: the decision to work rather than give up, to be faithful rather than untrustworthy, and to follow God rather than her own will. The same virtues should be seen in husbands. Even if our bodies and hearts are broken or our circumstances debilitating, we can be a support to our spouses by constantly leaning on God through prayer.

Dear Lord, we are not always at our strongest. You understand that life is hard. In the midst of this, please help us be a support to each other rather than a burden.

ALLEGIANCE

*Let us offer through Jesus a continual sacrifice of praise to God,
proclaiming our allegiance to his name.*

HEBREWS 13:15 NLT

Allegiance, also known as loyalty, commitment, fidelity, duty, and faithfulness. Where does your allegiance lie? Are you committed to God and his ways? Are you faithful to your spouse? Jesus Christ was so committed to us that he reconciled our disloyalty to him by laying down his own life. Now, he asks us to remain faithful to him.

What do we have to offer as thanks for his incredible gift? We get to praise his name, offer him our allegiance, and be loyal in our marriages. To dutifully stick to these things, it's important that we seek him daily and rely on his strength. Praise God that he's committed to us! Let's follow his example in our commitments to others.

Dear Lord, thank you for your grace and love which you lavishly bestow on us. We will forever praise your name, but we want to give you more than just our praise. We offer you our complete allegiance too.

FROM THE BEGINNING

This is the message that you heard from the beginning,
that we should love one another.
1 JOHN 3:11 NKJV

From beginning to end, the gospel message is one of love. It's a story of love's reconciliation and the love of the Savior for his bride, the church. In Romans, Paul says that love fulfills the law, and in this passage, we see that reaffirmed. John told his readers the simple standard to which their actions should be held.

No matter how much we tend to complicate things, everything we do to our spouses and to others can be judged by the standard of whether it was done in a spirit of love or selfishness. We have no excuse for any ill-considered, selfish action because we have heard this message "from the beginning, that we should love one another."

God, it's difficult to find sincere love in our hearts when we feel dry and parched inside and exhausted by the road behind us. Please give us the understanding and compassion to love one another in both the desert and the oasis. Specifically, may our love for each other mimic the love you never fail to show to your bride.

VALUE

Who can find a virtuous wife?
For her worth is far above rubies.
PROVERBS 31:10 NKJV

There are several places in the Scriptures that prize virtue and wisdom above the value of precious stones and great wealth. One of those places is the depiction of the famous Proverbs 31 woman. She has great wisdom, is industrious, and cares so deeply for her family that Solomon claims a wife like this is more valuable than rubies.

Many people use the Proverbs 31 Women as a benchmark to be achieved or aspired to, but the Bible is simply painting a picture of God's priorities once again. He is not impressed with the glittering riches that catch our eye. His heart is captivated by the one who is faithful to him, walks in his ways, and is a good steward of the people and possessions he has given them.

We want to be good wives and husbands, Father God. We want to be faithful to you and take good care of who and what you have given us. We want to be a blessing to each other; please show us how. Thank you.

All In

"If you refuse to take up your cross and follow me,
you are not worthy of being mine.
If you cling to your life, you will lose it;
but if you give up your life for me, you will find it."
MATTHEW 10:38-39 NLT

Anything worth doing is worth doing well. Anything that takes time, effort, and energy is worth our dedication and care because those things are costly. You can't get your time back if you lose it. It's hard to get back what has been lost to no good end. Most importantly, what is the point of getting engaged in something without going all in on it? This is what Jesus meant in this verse when he says anyone who does not take his cross and follow him is not worthy of him.

Just like our path in Christ, we have to stay focused on the goal when it comes to our marriage. We can't be halfhearted about it. It will be worth exactly what effort we put into it.

Lord, some things are worth all we have; our marriage is one of those things. Please make us willing to give all we are and all we have for our marriage to stand strong and thrive.

Valuing Relationships

God is faithful, by whom you were called into the fellowship of His Son, Jesus Christ our Lord.

1 Corinthians 1:9 NKJV

Paul explained to the Corinthian Christians that not only were they saved by faith in the Lord Jesus Christ, but they were also called into fellowship with him. Similarly, thousands of years later, we are called into the same fellowship. God did not save us just to add numbers to his kingdom; he saved us because he loves us and wants a relationship with each one of us. Relationship matters to God. He has no intention of being some distant deity or giving this sinful world a wide berth. In fact, he has gone to the greatest lengths to be near us and play an active role in our lives.

Marriage is a unique relationship that matters greatly to God. He designed it to give us a taste of the love he feels for us. Marriage is a valuable gift. How are you placing value on yours? How does it teach you about God's character?

Dearest Lord, thank you for saving us and for the relationship we have with you. We also thank you for the relationship we have with each other. Give us insight into the immense value these relationships hold so we truly appreciate them and do right by you and each other.

MAY

If a man tried to buy love

with all his wealth,

his offer would be utterly scorned.

SONG OF SOLOMON 8:7 NLT

Go to God

*"I pray, Lord God of heaven, O great and awesome God,
You who keep Your covenant and mercy with those who love You
and observe Your commandments."*

NEHEMIAH 1:5 NKJV

Our Father in heaven is faithful and intent on keeping the promises he made to us. Instead of attempting to sort out troubling circumstances on our own, we can pray to our infinite Creator. He will give us the answers we need.

Are you facing a difficult situation today? Before wading through it alone, bring it to God in prayer. When you run into difficulty in your marriage, God is happy to help. Let us not use our own strength to address important issues we face without first bringing them to the Lord in prayer, for there is no situation the Lord can't lead us through. There is no difficulty in life too puzzling for God.

Heavenly Father, thank you for the exemplary life of Nehemiah. He immediately turned to you in humble prayer when confronted with insurmountable difficulty. We want to do likewise today and not sidestep your sufficient provision or try to solve life's problems on our own. May your will be done in all circumstances.

The Greatest Sacrifice

"God so loved the world that he gave his one and only Son, that whoever believes in him shall not perish but have eternal life."
John 3:16 NIV

How does believing in God change the way you live? How does it affect the way you treat others? It's difficult to comprehend the full extent of the sacrifice Jesus made for us, but we can show our appreciation for his gift by sacrificing for others.

God trusted us with spouses and gave us the gift of life together. We can thank him by loving our partners, sacrificing for them, and encouraging them in their own walks with our Lord and Savior. May we always remember it was because of that terrible, wonderful, excruciating, life-giving moment on the cross that we're free to live, serve, and love. Let's make the most of it.

King Jesus, the gift you gave us can never be earned or repaid, but we can show you our gratitude by sharing it with others. We love you; help us follow you now and forever.

PARTNERSHIP

You husbands must give honor to your wives. Treat your wife with understanding as you live together. She may be weaker than you are, but she is your equal partner in God's gift of new life. Treat her as you should so your prayers will not be hindered.

1 PETER 3:7 NLT

For most people in the world and even some Christians, conversations about submitting cause negative reverberations in their minds. It can bring a master-servant of image to mind, but that is not at all what the Bible is speaking about in 1 Peter 3:7. The idea of a husband serving his wife goes hand-in-hand with the wife serving her husband. While she is supporting him and making his life better in all the ways the Lord lays on her heart, the husband is also considering his wife and thinking about ways he can make her life better. They are equal partners.

Being a team player in your marriage has nothing to do with a servant-master dynamic, but since we are sinful people, it's understandable that this is how many people interpret submission in a marriage. It is also why healthy, thriving marriages among Christians should be the norm so the lost world has a reference point for what healthy marriage looks like.

Lord, the lost world often gets confused about your Word, and even some believers get the wrong idea about how you have structured marriage. Your plan, however, is perfect, and all your instructions are wholesome. They bring health and not harm. May we be an example to the world as we trust your plan.

A New Command

"A new command I give you: Love one another.
As I have loved you, so you must love one another."
JOHN 13:34 NIV

The Old Testament has entire books on how to be righteous before God. It tells of the requirements for purity, cleanliness, and being acceptable in the presence of God. Those requirements, as true as they are, cannot be fulfilled by weak earthly creatures like ourselves. That is why God sent his Son, out of love, to die for us.

According to the New Testament, love fulfills the law. With his sacrifice, God fulfilled the law not by grain or burnt offerings but by a life defined by perfect love. When we act out of love, when we have concern for others above ourselves, and above them a concern for God, we are fulfilling the new command. This is the command God gave to us to fulfill the law. We can look at the way Jesus lived his life and the way he loved us as an example.

God, please teach us to love as you have loved. We want to follow your new command.

STRENGTH AND PATIENCE

We also pray that you will be strengthened with all his glorious power
so you will have all the endurance and patience you need.
May you be filled with joy.

COLOSSIANS 1:11 NLT

Relationships are tough. Anyone who has been married will tell you it requires patience and humility. Patience begins with an individual; we can't control our spouses, but we can control our actions and our reactions. Patience and wisdom include discerning what needs to be changed and what needs to be tolerated.

On the wedding day, we likely considered our spouses practically perfect in our love-struck eyes, but reality sets in eventually. We are all flawed humans. Thankfully, our Father in heaven gives us strength and patience to make godly, loving choices even when we don't feel like it. Like marriage itself, patience is the work of a lifetime. Each day brings new opportunities to cultivate this valuable virtue with joy.

Oh Lord, please strengthen us and give us patience by your glorious power. We know the point of marriage is not sameness but strength through unity. May we cherish the differences we see in each other.

IF YOU LOVE ME

"If you love Me, keep My commandments."
JOHN 14:15 NKJV

This is a bold statement from Jesus. He did not say most commandments or nearly all of them; he said, "my commandments." There is no qualification as to which ones are more required. Christ requires all of them be kept. This isn't possible, since we all sin and come short of God's glory, but it doesn't mean we should not try.

A spouse who focuses their life on keeping God's commands will find their love for Christ and for their significant other is above and beyond what they could have hoped for without God's guidelines. God loves love because it requires the best of us: the perfection of character through commitment and humility. In his love and mercy, he also gave the blood of his Son to wash away every moment where we fail to keep Jesus' commandments.

Oh Jesus, how great is the measure of love you gave us on the cross and through your life. Without you, we have no power to follow your commands or grow in your love. Please give us your strength and righteousness to do what we cannot do on our own.

PERSISTENCE IN PRAYER

The LORD hears his people when they call to him for help.
He rescues them from all their troubles.

PSALM 34:17 NLT

It's easy to give up on prayer when we don't experience answers or results in the timeframe we anticipated. We tend to feel hopeless when we don't believe help will come. As children of God, we need never feel hopeless because help will always come. The journey may not be the easiest or most comfortable. God may seem silent or the path unbearable, but if you pray to God, he most definitely hears and will always deliver you.

What troubles are you facing today? Have you been praying about them for a long time? Keep praying, dear friend. The Lord hears you, and he will certainly rescue you from all your troubles.

Dearest Lord God, thank you for each new day you give us. Today, we will be hopeful and persistent in our prayers. Keep us confident in your promise that you hear us and will answer in your perfect timing. You are our rescue and reward.

Intimate

His left hand is under my head,
And his right hand embraces me.

Song of Solomon 8:3 NKJV

There is a love, pure and intimate, that cares genuinely for another person. Picture two lovers: his arm is under her head because they are facing each other. Their focus is on each other. He embraces her because they are comfortable and close together. The love they share isn't self-seeking; its interest and concern is for the other person.

This is the kind of love Christ has for us. He even laid down his own life for our sake. This is the kind of love he wants us to experience with each other. Our marriage can be intimate, comfortable, and focused on one another because that is the love Christ gives us and teaches us to give to each other.

We love you so dearly, Lord Jesus. Thank you for your intimate, sacrificial love. Please bless our marriage and teach us to love like you.

Not Captive

See to it that no one takes you captive by philosophy and empty deceit, according to human tradition, according to the elemental spirits of the world, and not according to Christ.

Colossians 2:8 esv

All around us and at every turn, influences try to pull us in their direction. Sometimes an argument may sound compelling, but once put into practice, it bears no good fruit. This is why we're told to test all things. It doesn't mean to be argumentative since we're also told to pursue peace, but we must question so we're not easily ensnared.

If we have hidden God's Word in our hearts, then we will know what is true; we can't be lied to or caught off guard. Having a lifestyle of truth, spending time often with God, and studying the Scriptures is the best way to stay free and not be taken captive by empty philosophy and deceit. Remember, just because everyone else is doing it doesn't make it right.

Dear Jesus, guide us and shine a light on the path you want us to follow. We committed our lives to you; please teach us to walk in that commitment daily and learn from your influence. Nurture our knowledge of the Scriptures and keep us from becoming ensnared by flowery words and falsities.

Expansive Love

Your love, Lord, reaches to the heavens,
your faithfulness to the skies.
Your righteousness is like the highest mountains,
your justice like the great deep.
You, Lord, preserve both people and animals.

Psalm 36:5-6 niv

What is God's love like? The psalmist draws a comparison to the greatest expanse he can think of: the heavens. God is a great and glorious God. In him is the perfection of all human emotion as its heavenly counterpart. Just as heaven is infinite in time, God's attributes are infinite in their magnitude. Our love is a drop in the bucket compared to the ocean of God's love. Even an ocean is too small to portray his depth and breadth of emotion.

His righteousness, justice, and faithfulness are similarly unending. In fact, his faithfulness is so great, he remains faithful to us even when we are not faithful because he can't deny who he is. It is a fortunate and glorious thing that God's heart is inclined toward our needs and that he cares for us. What is our love and commitment in comparison to the unending love and faithfulness of God?

Oh Lord, make us faithful just as you are faithful. Make us love as you love. Make out of us a microscopic reflection of your magnitude and glory, and may we turn others' hearts toward you.

LIVING AGAINST TENSION

*Rejoice in hope, be patient in tribulation,
be constant in prayer.*

ROMANS 12:12 ESV

We should expect life to push against us. We are children of the King living in enemy territory. The devil does not want us to flourish in our faith; he wants to crush us. Once we get past the idea that this world should be easier, we find the truth of God's plan for our lives.

God wants us to live in the tension. He wants us to push back, to have hope in hopeless circumstances, strength in him when we are weak, and constancy in prayer when life is easy. He wants us to fight the circumstances that try to shape us into the image of the world. That is his desire for our spirits. That is how we will find ourselves molding to the image of the Son of God. In marital tensions, we are to love when we feel unloved. We are to be patient when filled with anger. We are to be the better version of our nature when we would rather not be. Embrace the tension.

Lord, help us to live against the tension of life today. By your great power, strengthen us to fight against the sin within.

STRENGTH AND COURAGE

"Be strong and do not lose courage,
for there is a reward for your work."
2 CHRONICLES 15:7 NASB

In the Lord, the strong and courageous are those who seek God when they wake up, who serve their families, who are faithful to their spouses, and who share generously with those who need it. The strong and courageous are those who will not be deterred by trivial tasks, petty issues, or the bad behavior of those around them. The strong and courageous are men and women who choose God when everyone else is going the other direction, who sacrifice now for a better reward later, and who care for the needs of others even if those they serve can never return the favor.

God defines strength and courage differently than the world does, and he promises they will be rewarded in the end. God's rewards are also very different, and much better, than the world's rewards.

When moments require it, Lord God, please help us be strong and courageous. We want to honor you with our lives.

CHILDREN OF GOD

See how great a love the Father has given us, that we would be called children of God; and in fact we are. For this reason the world does not know us: because it did not know Him.

1 JOHN 3:1 NASB

We have been given the very nature of God. Because he saved us from our sinful nature and brought us into his family, we are his children and heirs. As we spend time with him, we become more like him and less like the worldly influences around us.

The people we spend time with influence us and craft our characters, so it is important we spend quality time with God. There are many voices out there, but as children of God, we need to listen to the voice of our Father above all others. When we do, we can better understand the love he has put in us, the calling he has placed on us, and the people he is shaping us to be.

We are your loving children, heavenly Father, and we want nothing more than to spend time in your presence and become more like you. As you nurture us, please grow our marriage too. We want the onlooking world to notice it is different; it is a union committed to you and your ways.

WINNING

We do not lose heart. Though outwardly we are wasting away,
yet inwardly we are being renewed day by day. For our light and
momentary troubles are achieving for us an eternal glory
that far outweighs them all.

2 CORINTHIANS 4:16-17 NIV

Even when it looks like we are losing, we are always winning with God. What a glorious promise! Imagine you've been bringing up the rear in a tough marathon. In the last moments, you have an unyielding strength, and you beat out the exhausted competition to win the race.

The grind is difficult and the path steep, but the Bible promises that even though our bodies waste away, God is renewing us every day. He gives us fresh strength, new hope, refined wisdom, and a deeper knowledge of him. The glory to come outshines any suffering or hardship we're currently undergoing. Keep pressing on, don't lose heart, and hold on to your faith. It will only get better with time.

Dear Lord, thank you for the courage you give us each day. We are grateful that even though life gets tough at times, you renew us daily by giving us spiritual strength and eternal glory.

THE LORD'S DIRECTION

*May the Lord direct your hearts into the love of God
and into the patience of Christ.*

2 THESSALONIANS 3:5 NKJV

We can't bring our own hearts to God in humility. We can't bring anything to God without his help. He loved us first, he sought us first, he is always the one to act and give. It's the same with love and commitment. Here, Paul prays for the Lord to direct the hearts of his listeners back to the love of God and the steadfastness of Christ.

Only the Lord can direct us, and we can pray he directs us to the love and steadfastness only he can supply. We can't base our commitment to someone on our flawed character or actions and expect it to flourish. We must base our relationships on hope in the Lord and ask him to make us vessels of his faithfulness and loyalty. Thankfully, he is always willing to do so; it brings him glory and is in line with the character of his heart. All we need do is ask, ask again, and pray every day for the faithfulness only God can supply.

Great and gracious Lord Jesus, lead our hearts to your love and steadfastness. Give us the virtues we can't continuously muster on our own. Please pour into us your character of loyalty.

DIFFERENT GIFTS

*Since we have gifts that differ according to the grace given to us,
each of us is to use them properly.*
ROMANS 12:6 NASB

Can you image if your spouse was exactly like you? Where would be the fun in that? Marriages push and pull and stretch us. They teach us to live for someone else and with someone else. They reveal our weaknesses and call on our strengths.

God made us different for two reasons. First, we complement each other better. We have someone to help where we're weak, and we can use our strengths to help them. Second, we are made in the image of God, and different people display different aspects of his character. God's character is endless, and we are his children. He may reveal the gift of teaching in one, the gift of music in another, and the gift of organization in someone else. He diversifies and then tells us to work together. Let's remember how important and special each person is and refuse the temptation to compare; that can lead to jealousy or pride. The body functions best when we work together. In the same way, marriage will function best when we appreciate the balance the other person brings.

Thank you for giving each of us different gifts, Lord God. Show us ways to appreciate them in each other and how to use them well.

GOOD THOUGHTS

I remember the days of old;
I meditate on all that you have done;
I ponder the work of your hands.

PSALM 143:5 ESV

What can we think about? There is much to choose from. The mind is the window to the soul, and it can let in the darkest night or the brightest light. The psalmist of this passage has a window letting in the light of God's Word and works. He is encouraged by what God has accomplished. He is aware of God's nature as seen since "the days of old." Thoughts like these don't come naturally for humans, but they can be learned through transformative experiences and much, much prayer. If neglected, the window to the soul turns dark with resentment, unforgiveness, and apathy. If left to our own devices, we easily lose sight of God's grace for us.

A spouse is usually the closest person to their partner's soul. They are most affected by its condition, and they can tell when their spouse spiritually broken. If our spouses warn us of spiritual darkness, we should consider the state of our hearts and minds.

Lord, give us the thoughts of the psalmist. Let these thoughts fill us with gratitude, commitment, and love. Keep us alert to the state of our souls.

SOUND JUDGMENT

Whoever isolates himself seeks his own desire;
he breaks out against all sound judgment.
PROVERBS 18:1 ESV

Living with people is tough but living alone is tougher. We can live alone and isolate, even in a room full of people, by not allowing anyone into our thoughts or feelings. We were meant to live in community and share our space, including our mental space, and to work though relationship issues. Problems will arise, but God has given us everything we need to work through conflict for the purpose of peace and growth. He grants sound judgment and wisdom to those who seek him.

Isolating ourselves invites all sorts of problems because we are left without other perspectives, encouragement, accountability, or important reminders. It may seem easier to avoid inevitable problems, but relationships are worth the extra work.

God, we pray for our marriage specifically today. Help us be vulnerable with each other and not isolate. Walk with us as we navigate our problems. Please give us the wisdom and sound judgment we need.

BAD BEHAVIOR

Keep a good conscience so that in the thing in which you are slandered, those who disparage your good behavior in Christ will be put to shame.

1 PETER 3:16 NASB

This passage warns us to be mindful of our behavior and not give anyone a reason to accuse us. If we have nothing to hide and no bad record to point to, anyone who comes against us will be the one put to shame and not us.

But what about in your marriage? What about your spouse who knows more about you than anyone? Nobody knows your ugly side as well as your spouse. They see you at your best and your worst. We all need a safe place to let our walls down, but in truth, we still need to be on our best behavior with our spouses. After all, they deserve it more than anyone else.

We pray for help, Lord God, in how we act toward each other. We want our marriage to reflect your love and not become an ugly game of accusations. Help us as we strive to offer each other the very best versions of ourselves. Give us extra grace to not hold any past sins against each other.

THOUGHT LIFE

Whatever is true, whatever is honorable, whatever is right, whatever is pure, whatever is lovely, whatever is commendable, if there is any excellence and if anything worthy of praise, think about these things.
PHILIPPIANS 4:8 NASB

The mind is the starting point for behavior. When the evil one wants to entice a person to sin, he starts in their mind. He speaks lies and condemnation until he gets the emotional response he is looking for. When anxious thoughts flood our minds or we are tempted to sin, our immediate reaction should be to look to Jesus and remember who we are in Christ.

As married people, it's even more important that we channel godly thoughts since our emotions have an acute effect on someone else too. As spouses, we are in a perfect position to hold each other accountable, encourage each other, and pray for the thought life of one another.

Almighty God, the more we think about you and the wonderful attributes connected to you, the more captivated and encouraged we become. Please keep anxiety at bay and remind us to pray for each other. Knowing that the light of Christ and the darkness of evil cannot abide together, we want to make a conscious choice to meditate on things worthy of praise.

CONTENTMENT

I know what it is to be in need, and I know what it is to have plenty. I have learned the secret of being content in any and every situation, whether well fed or hungry, whether living in plenty or in want.

PHILIPPIANS 4:12 NIV

Are there things you believe you need to be happy and content? Maybe it's a job position or a certain house. Maybe it's having children or a certain amount in your savings account. Whatever it is, the truth is the only thing that will satisfy your soul and calm the longing in your heart is your relationship with God.

The world constantly tells us what we "need." Sometimes, we have honest, godly desires. However evil or noble our yearnings are, they will never bring contentment. When we fill our hearts with God, reveling in all he has done and praising his incredible character, we are participating in the exact act we were created for, and our souls will recognize it. Everything else vying for our attention will grow dim, and our earthly desires will no longer be able to overwhelm us.

Please help us find perfect contentment in you alone, Lord Jesus. Our souls know that only you can satisfy, but our eyes often get distracted. Fill us up with your love today, we pray, as we sit here with you.

BE STILL

"The LORD will fight for you;
you need only to be still."
EXODUS 14:14 NIV

Surrendering to God can be a difficult thing to muster. His timing is not our timing, and often we become impatient and attempt to take matters into our own hands. The Bible is full of individuals who tried to force God's hand or rush his plan. It's hard to drop an offense or move past a wrongdoing without trying to enact our own imperfect version of justice.

God, however, sees the big picture where we only have our temporary, linear perspective. Far better would it be for us and everyone else involved if we trusted God to do what he promised he would. When our rights are denied us and we feel infringed upon, we can have peace knowing that God will fight for us.

God of Justice, we know that perfect judgment is higher than our paygrade as humans. Please have grace on us as we learn to surrender to you and be patient. Your timing and judgments are flawless.

GOOD WORK

Let us not become weary in doing good,
for at the proper time we will reap a harvest
if we do not give up.
GALATIANS 6:9 NIV

Doing good work is hard, especially if you begin to doubt if it matters. We can toil for months or years without seeing anything change, and it's easy to grow weary. Paul knew this, so he urged the Galatians to keep living in a way that was consistent with what they believed. They were free people in Christ, and God's Spirit was with them. Eventually, a crop of eternal worth would grow if they kept up their good work.

Often God will show his people how their efforts matter, but sometimes he won't. When you don't see immediate growth, are you prepared to keep planting? When days are hard and you are tired, can you keep up the good work knowing that your reward is coming?

We ask you for daily strength, heavenly Father. We sometimes feel we don't have what it takes to continue. Please renew us to do your work. We know it will be worthwhile in the end. In fact, it will be the only thing that matters.

Repent

"Repent of your sins and turn to God,
for the Kingdom of Heaven is near."
MATTHEW 3:2 NLT

Matthew takes the coming of the kingdom of heaven very seriously; he instructs his readers more than thirty times to repent. The repentance he refers to is not just admitting our sins to God and asking for his forgiveness. It means going to him truly broken and asking him to help us change. Sin separates us from God, and that is the most heartbreaking issue of all. When we turn to God, we turn away from our sins.

Furthermore, God's kingdom is not a fairy tale or an unreachable idea. It is a real, thriving kingdom nearer than we realize. We can't know when we will end our time here and wake up there; none of us are told how many days we are given. God sees the big picture where we see only a temporary, linear perspective. It doesn't work to plan to repent later after we've had our unrighteous fun. God wants our hearts, allegiance, and obedience here and now. Today is the day to turn and repent.

Dear God, please help us turn away from our sin and face you instead. You have given each of us an unknown number of days, and we don't want to waste them unrepentant. Living for you is so much better and brighter. Thank you for accepting us in our broken states and helping us heal and change.

RESTORATION

*When they had finished breakfast, Jesus said to Simon
Peter, "Simon, son of John, do you love me more than these?"
He said to him, "Yes, Lord; you know that I love you."
He said to him, "Feed my lambs."*
JOHN 21:15 ESV

There is much to glean from this encounter between Jesus and
Peter. Peter had messed up. In his Lord's most difficult moments,
Peter abandoned him. It was a terrible betrayal, but it was not a
surprise to Jesus. He knew Peter would let him down, yet he chose
to call him anyway. He knew Peter would never be able to love him
back as much he loved Peter, but he loved him still.

Like Peter, we let Jesus down all the time. We fail to measure up,
but that doesn't come as a surprise to Jesus. He knew we would
fail, but he chose to love us, save us, and help us anyway. The most
amazing part of this story is the completeness of Jesus' forgiveness
as he fully embraced Peter and reinstated his discipleship. Don't be
deterred when you fail. Take Jesus' hand, get back up, and try again.

When we fail, faithful Lord, please help us get back up.
When we go astray, lead us back to you. Thank you
for loving us even while knowing we often mess up.
We will be faithful to learn from our falls and continue
feeding your sheep.

DEPENDENCY

The LORD protects those of childlike faith;
I was facing death, and he saved me.

PSALM 116:6 NLT

Our society is deeply individualistic. The most-praised people don't need anybody, lean on themselves, and are self-made. Even in the culture of relationships, the worst people are the ones who are painted bothersome or intrusive or who stop by unannounced. Everyone wants to be left alone.

In God's eyes, the greatest people are children because they are the most dependent. They know they can't make it on their own and that they need a parent to help them. God wants us to be his children. He wants to be our helper and hear us "sing for joy in the shadow of [God's] wings" (Ps 63:6). He wants to occupy our thoughts, so we lie awake thinking about him and meditate on him throughout the night. That is his desire for us. If we are to be supportive and reliable for our spouse, we do not need independence; we need heavy dependence on God.

God, we are a couple dependent on you. In the mornings and the evenings, teach us to lean on you and rely on you. Occupy our minds, Lord, and be our primary thought. Thank you for saving us.

Eyes of Light

"The eye is the lamp of the body.
So, if your eye is healthy, your whole body will be full of light."
MATTHEW 6:22 ESV

We can't keep up a façade for long because our eyes will betray us. If we're pretending to be okay but we're not, if we have hidden sin, or if we haven't been spending time with God, our whole temperament will darken. It will be revealed in the way we walk, talk, and live. Our smiles and our eyes will change.

On the other hand, when we walk in the light and set up accountability, when we're healthy and happy, and when we spend intentional time with God, our auras will be more joyful and light. Others will notice, either consciously or subconsciously, that we're different. Our spouses will definitely be able to tell, so if they mention it, we would be wise to take note.

Jesus, please fill us with your light as we study your Word and walk in your ways. We want to experience your blessings and also be a blessing to others.

FRIENDSHIP

Many will say they are loyal friends,
but who can find one who is truly reliable?
The godly walk with integrity;
blessed are their children who follow them.

PROVERBS 20:6-7 NLT

Regardless of whether your relationship with your spouse began as a friendship or not, it's important to cultivate a friendship with them now. How you value each other within your marriage forms how the two of you communicate. Good friends respect each other even when they disagree. Good friends want the best for each other and feel proud, not threatened, when the other person succeeds.

As Christians, it's especially important that we watch our words and treat each other with love and respect because that is how we have been treated, and we know it's the better way. Reliability and integrity will be game changers for your marriage and all your relationships.

Thank you for this great friendship, God, and for uniting us together in marriage. Please help us mature in our relationship even more and truly enjoy it. We recognize that you have entrusted us, your children, to each other, and we promise to treat each other with integrity and respect.

ACTING BY COMMAND

"Whoever has my commands and keeps them is the one who loves me. The one who loves me will be loved by my Father, and I too will love them and show myself to them."

JOHN 14:21 NIV

In this passage from John, we see Jesus' diagnosis for love. In his eyes, love is evidenced through devotion to God and his ways. He says that to love him, we must have his commandments and keep them. Not only is this an action of love, but it is also an action deserving of God's love and favor. Jesus says, "The one who loves me will be loved by my Father, and I too will love them." There is no condition on Christ's love, nor can we earn it, but those who take up their cross and love God will find his heart open and his love pouring down on them.

This is God's command: live by devotion and humility while looking to him for guidance. This is not done out of compulsion but out of love for God and a desire to do his will. This way of living brings us peace in home and at work and helps us endure life's struggles.

God, help us live by your commands to love you and seek to please you. Guide us to your way in the midst of many other ways presented to us.

STRONGER TOGETHER

A person standing alone can be attacked and defeated,
but two can stand back-to-back and conquer.
Three are even better, for a triple-braided cord is not easily broken.
ECCLESIASTES 4:12 NLT

One of the greatest things about marriage is that you have a teammate. Throughout your life, you have someone to watch out for your interests and have your back. Life is easier when you have a close partner to go through everything together, to hold on to during dark days and nights, and to fight alongside you when your strength is sapped. When you feel like you can't keep going, a mate makes all the difference.

Four hands are better than two; two heads can solve a problem quicker than one. We are meant to rely on each other. Each of us have unique and important strengths that we bring into marriage. When combined with our third partner, God, we become a powerful team equipped to deal with what life may throw our way.

Lord, in unity there is strength, and two are better than one. We thank you for the strength found in the union of marriage. Keep us in harmony through your Spirit as you are united with us through Christ. Let us grow strong enough to overcome any challenges in our Christian life and marriage.

DIVINELY SANCTIONED

*"What therefore God has joined together,
let not man separate."*

MARK 10:9 ESV

Marriage is not a human concept. It's God's idea, and God's plan for marriage is both a blessing and a challenge. The world has lost the meaning of marriage in that so many people treat it with a casual attitude. Marriage is serious; it is not to be trifled with. As we read in Mark 10:9, "What God has joined together, let no one separate."

In a world that is largely self-serving, we can stray from this truth by putting ourselves before God. Through prayer and reading the Word, believers can keep their eyes on the prize of a blessed and fruitful marriage. We don't want to miss the goodness in store for those who are faithful to him and to their marriage.

Lord, thank you for the gift of marriage. We know it's not a man's idea; it comes directly from you. Your plan allows us to live out our marriage in a way that honors you. Let us be people who seek to bring reconciliation and not discord. Instead of disunity, let us bring healing and wholeness to marriage.

June

Love is supreme and must flow through
each of these virtues. Love becomes the
mark of true maturiy.

COLOSSIANS 3:14 TPT

Unity in Marriage

Make my joy complete by being of the same mind,
maintaining the same love, united in spirit,
intent on one purpose.
PHILIPPIANS 2:2 NASB

For believers to be united in love, we must let the mind of Christ dwell in us richly and display the same beautiful disposition that Jesus displayed during his earthly life. It is all the more important for married couples to strive toward being like-minded and united in love and purpose. They are joined as one and are lifelong partners in the work of the gospel.

Together with our spouses, let's commit to growing and maturing in our faith. Only as we are transformed into the likeness of Christ, by the power of the Holy Spirit, will we be able to discern what is of God and display it in our lives.

Oh, what joy there is in being united in love, purpose, and spirit! We praise you, Father, for our marriage, our physical family, our family of believers, and most of all our relationship with you. May we bring you joy by striving for peace and unity within our marriage.

WISDOM

If any of you lacks wisdom, let him ask God,
who gives generously to all without reproach,
and it will be given him.
JAMES 1:5 ESV

Are you at a crossroads and don't know which way to go? Perhaps you feel stuck in life. Are relationships difficult for you? Maybe you want to understand the character of God better. Whatever you need wisdom or discernment for, God wants to give it to you. That does not mean he will give you the answer to every question, but true wisdom is coupled with contentment and trust. Wisdom knows the difference between righteousness and good-looking worldliness. Wisdom considers the long-term consequences of a decision instead of immediate gratification.

If you are struggling with this sort of perspective, go to God. Ask him for his discernment. He will gladly give you everything you need.

You are where true wisdom is found, almighty God. Please give us the wisdom we need as we seek you today. Bless our marriage with love, wisdom, contentment, and trust.

No Fear

There is no fear in love, but perfect love drives out fear, because fear involves punishment, and the one who fears is not perfected in love.

1 John 4:18 NASB

Love is as opposed to fear as oil is to water. The two don't mix; they don't allow for each other's presence in the same space. When people are afraid, they often look to confidence, anger, or aggression to break their fear, but John tells us, "perfect love drives out fear." We can only live in love when we live in the knowledge that Jesus loves us. If he loves us, and we know he does, then there is no rational expectation of punishment. The punishment is paid for and done.

When we are finally perfected in love, we will perfectly love God, perfectly comprehend his love for us, and be devoid of fear. If he loves us, he will provide for us. If he loves our spouse and children, he will provide for them too. His love is a provisioning love that washes away our fear of abandonment, need, and insecurity.

Dear God, cast out the demons of fear and anxiety. Give us faith and understanding of your unbreakable love for us. You will never let us go and never fail us. Help us stand firm in this trust.

Living Redeemed

Show yourself in all respects to be a model of good works, and in your teaching show integrity, dignity, and sound speech that cannot be condemned, so that an opponent may be put to shame, having nothing evil to say about us.

Titus 2:7-8 esv

A believer's life is different from a person not submitted to the will of Christ, and a marriage between believers will reflect that. As believers, we are often the way unbelievers learn about Christ and his message. Our lives are not perfect, but they should definitely look different.

Unbelievers should see us, as married Christians, favoring our spouse to ourselves, making decisions together for the glory of God, and running to God for help when we need it. We should be quick to apologize and quick to forgive. Others should see us filled with peace during difficult times and asking God for answers when we don't have them. We should be humble, prayerful, and genuine. When we mess up and admit it, seeking forgiveness or help, it shows others not that we're perfect but that we are redeemed.

Oh God, our intention is not to pretend we're perfect because we're Christians; everyone knows we're flawed. We want others to see your perfection through us! You had grace on us, the guilty, and now our lives look different because of you.

SHIFTING CIRCUMSTANCES

I have learned to be content
whatever the circumstances.
PHILIPPIANS 4:11 NIV

Do you know the difference between contentment and having a life filled with good things? Contentment is not found in anything external but in the condition of your heart. Things come and go, but God's love is forever. Instead of creating the life you always wanted, first become the type of person who stands on God's truth and can weather any storm. Then, if the waves sweep through and carry away everything you love, it may shake you, but you will not fall.

External forces, like loss of people or possessions, may influence you, but they can't change who you are unless you allow it. Learn to have a content spirit by filling your heart with God's goodness, and nothing will steal that from you. How can you work on contentment today with your spouse? As strong as you'd be alone with God, you'll be even stronger together with God.

Father, teach us contentment in life, our marriage, our jobs, and in every area of life. Before working on our living conditions, we choose to work on the conditions of our hearts.

HIGHER CALLING

"If you love those who love you, what credit is that to you? For even sinners love those who love them. And if you do good to those who do good to you, what credit is that to you? For even sinners do the same."

LUKE 6:32-33 NASB

We naturally gravitate toward relationships with something to offer us. Have you ever had to love someone who hated you or serve someone who has never lifted a finger for you? Sometimes God calls us to serve the spiteful and love the unloving. Have you found yourself in a situation like that? How did you embrace it?

It's easy to love the people who love us, but God loves even those who curse him. Because we love God, we love what God loves. You will also encounter bad days with those who do love you, like your spouse, when they aren't acting kind or loving. Does the balance feel off? Stop thinking about what's fair and don't assume that love is only a feeling. Follow the example of your Savior and choose love.

Loving Father, we are so thankful that life isn't fair. We know what we deserve, yet you atoned us. Because of your great love for us, we can love and serve others even when it isn't fair, we don't feel like it, or we know they can never repay us.

FORGIVENESS

*"When you stand praying, if you hold anything against anyone,
forgive them, so that your Father in heaven may forgive you your sins."*

MARK 11:25 NIV

If you've lived on this earth for any amount of time, someone
at some point has wronged you. You've been insulted, taken
advantage of, rejected, inconvenienced, and the list goes on. Dear
Christian, hear this: the Lord understands, If anyone knows what it
is like to be hurt, it's the Lord. If you need strength today to forgive,
ask him for that strength because he will give it to you. He has a lot
of practice forgiving us of our plethora of sins.

It's hard to forgive, but it's also a requirement. In light of all the Lord
has done, he doesn't require much of us, but he does require us to
forgive others. It's not easy, but it is absolutely necessary if we want
God to forgive us.

Thank you for forgiving us over and over again, Father.
We need your help today to forgive others. Sometimes
we need to forgive each other, sometimes ourselves,
sometimes a stranger who cuts us off in traffic, and
sometimes a deep and hidden wound someone inflicted
in our past. In all instances, please help us find the
strength to forgive.

OUR TRUE DESIRE

Whoever desires to love life and see good days, let him keep his tongue from evil and his lips from speaking deceit; let him turn away from evil and do good; let him seek peace and pursue it.

1 PETER 3:10-11 ESV

Our true desires come out when we are given choices. We can say that we "love life" and desire "good days," but if we are given the choice to gossip or speak to our favor rather than to the truth, what will we do? Will the decision reflect what we said our values are? "Speaking deceit" entails more than lying; bending the truth, manipulating others through phrasing, and even using the fine print on a contract to an unfair advantage are all deceitful.

This is the evil God wants us to keep from our lips. The people who love life and experience good in their relationships, people who are envied the most, make the difficult choices. They choose to not gossip when they rather would. They choose to elevate others with their speech rather than themselves. This is the pattern of conduct God wants us to commit to.

Dear God, train us and turn our patterns of speech toward you. Help us "seek peace and pursue it."

Ultimate Satisfaction

Surely goodness and mercy shall follow me
All the days of my life;
And I will dwell in the house of the Lord
Forever.

Psalm 23:6 nkjv

Our bodies and minds naturally crave comfort. We seek comfortable circumstances for our own good every way we turn. It takes active thinking and dedication to push outside our comfort zone, and such thinking and dedication makes us grow. God does not have an eternity of struggle and change destined for us. He has a big house with many rooms and an eternity of fellowship with him. He ultimately wants to give us a life of comfort, which is strange for many Christians to think about.

In the psalmist David's eyes, "all the days" of his life are filled with goodness and mercy on his path. However, this same man was often filled with pessimism and despair. It was only on occasion that the clouds cleared, and he could see God's ultimate providence and grace in his life. The same is true of us. We can hope and relax in the knowledge that, while we must struggle to see God's grace in this life, it will be always before our eyes in eternity.

God, give us hope this day in our ultimate comfort in you. Make us optimistic in light of our salvation.

KINGDOM LIVING

He died for all, so that those who live would no longer live for themselves, but for Him who died and rose on their behalf.

2 CORINTHIANS 5:15 NASB

Being a Christian is more than a cultural identifier or a moral indicator. It's more than a political adherence or an inherited tradition. Christ died for everyone, and salvation is a gift of grace available to anyone who accepts it and submits to Jesus Christ as Lord. We who live, we who have by grace received his resurrected life, should no longer live for ourselves but for our Lord and Savior.

May this come to mind every time we struggle to love our spouse, we struggle to forgive, or we want to insist on our own way. Let's remember what it means to be a Christian. Remember what Christ was willing to do for us.

Loving Lord and heavenly Savior, what glories are within your finished work of reconciliation. Thank you for saving us from ourselves. Thank you for the eternal life you have given us through your resurrection.

PEOPLE OF GOD

You, O man of God, flee these things and pursue righteousness,
godliness, faith, love, patience, gentleness.

1 TIMOTHY 6:11 NKJV

Paul calls Timothy a "man of God" here. To be a man or a woman of God is a difficult concept to grapple with. Many Christians do not grapple with it nearly enough. We put up caricatures of what manhood or womanhood should look like, but most of what we see and hear are influenced by romantic ideals more than biblical truth.

In this verse, we see the strong, "manly" qualities of righteousness, godliness, and faith, but that is only half of the coin. Men should also pursue love, patience, and gentleness. There is always a balance of virtues in God's plan. The same is true of women; the picture painted in Proverbs 31 describes virtues that balance each other in power and gentleness. In our marriages, we can slide into a false sense of manhood or womanhood based on non-biblical truth, but this passage brings us back to what it means to be people of God.

Dear God, create in us the perfect unity of strength, meekness, industry, and patience. Build in us the Spirit of God.

CARING FOR EACH OTHER

Do not merely look out for your own personal interests,
but also for the interests of others.

PHILIPPIANS 2:4 NASB

Selfless love is something most people aspire to, especially people who profess to follow Christ. Selfless love is particularly important to married people because it is that much more pertinent in day-to-day life and ministry. Remember, ministry starts in our homes first and then spreads outward. At the heart of marriage is the idea of being selfless and putting our spouses' needs before our own.

It is human nature to be self-serving, but thanks to the grace of God, he enables us to grow beyond our human abilities and become more like him. Let's learn from his example and aspire to love our spouses the same way he loves us.

Lord, we are grateful for your love and guidance in our marriage and for the example of Christ who gave his life to redeem us. Please open our eyes and hearts to each other's needs. Help us love and care for each other selflessly.

Unfair Trade

*God showed his great love for us by sending Christ
to die for us while we were still sinners.*

Romans 5:8 NLT

Have you ever suffered from buyer's remorse? Something caught your eye, and you were sure it would improve your life in some way. You bought it only to later realize it wasn't as life changing as you believed it would be.

Since the beginning of time, has anyone paid a higher price than Christ did for our forgiveness? And what a horrible value he got: the blood of the perfect Savior in exchange for the redemption of sinners. Still, he didn't regret his sacrifice. He decided we were worth it, not because of anything great we have done, but because he loves us.

It amazes us, dear Jesus, that you would exchange your precious life for ours while we were still lost in sin. In your love, you looked past our sin and saw the beloved children whom you created. Thank you forever and ever, Lord.

SELF-CONTROL

One who is slow to anger is better than the mighty,
And one who rules his spirit, than one who captures a city.
PROVERBS 16:32 NASB

All humans seek control. We are constantly subject to circumstances beyond our control, and this increases our desire to gain control over the world around us. When our control is threatened or things go against our will, we might lash out in anger or emotionally break down. We use all our might to convince others why they are wrong, why we are hurt, why we need more respect, or why our circumstances are unfair.

The writer of Proverbs shows us what we can control: our temperament. That is something we can dictate through God's power. Self-control is a power of the spirit and more valuable than the power of the body. According to this passage, we should seek to rule ourselves before we seek to rule anybody else. Self-control is often as valuable as love in our relationships. It keeps those around us safe; they don't become victims of our anger. More than that, it gives us direction and helps us accomplish what honors God.

Lord, increase in us self-control. Before we control our circumstances, may we control ourselves. May we control our own spirits.

FREEDOM TO SERVE

You were called to freedom, brothers and sisters;
only do not turn your freedom into an opportunity for the flesh,
but serve one another through love.
GALATIANS 5:13 NASB

The freedom we have been given through Christ is not intended for sin. We shouldn't willfully sin because we can just ask for forgiveness later. No, this freedom was given to us so we could serve one another. It insults God and his generosity to use this incredible, undeserved freedom to indulge in worldly and carnal activities which are in opposition to God's goodness.

We are to live as Christ lived: in holiness and righteousness, loving and serving the same way he did. The best place to start is with our own spouses since Christ also came to make a way for his bride, the church.

Father God, thank you for this important reminder that both legalism and a license to sin are unacceptable in the Christian life. We praise you for the freedom we have in Christ, and we will demonstrate our gratefulness in the ways we love and serve each other.

ABIDE WITH ME

"As the Father has loved me, so have I loved you. Now remain in my love. If you keep my commands, you will remain in my love, just as I have kept my Father's commands and remain in his love."

JOHN 15:9-10 NIV

This passage from John attests to our need to stay close to God and keep his commandments in order to abide in him. We depend on him to love us with a sustaining love. We live in his love every day, and through his love we find our source of love for others. We need to be connected to the source. If we are disconnected, we will wither away and be cut off.

The love we have for each other comes from God, and he enables us to be more selfless with our love just as the Scriptures say. The love we offer will be purer, more selfless, and more giving because it comes from being connected to God and abiding in him.

Lord, thank you for the blessing of your love. Through you, we learn what love looks like and how it helps us to be always connected to you. As we live in your will and walk this marriage path, may our love for each other increase each day because of you.

THE CHRISTIAN LIFE

We have not stopped praying for you since we first heard about you.
We ask God to give you complete knowledge of his will and to give
you spiritual wisdom and understanding. Then the way you live will
always honor and please the Lord, and your lives will produce every
kind of good fruit. All the while, you will grow as you learn to know
God better and better.

COLOSSIANS 1:9-10 NLT

God doesn't give us challenges or tests too difficult to figure out. The devil creates confusion, but God brings clarity. He gives us wisdom whenever we need it, and he sends his Holy Spirit to lead us through the chaos and comfort our hearts along the way.

Acting in love toward each other is the greatest way we can thank God and show him how abundantly grateful and committed we are to him. We show him love by loving his people. This is what it means to live honorably in a way that pleases God. Loving others, trusting him to guide us, and bearing fruit: that is what it looks like to truly follow the Lord.

Dear Father, we want to live honorably and be pleasing to you. Thank you for leading us, comforting us, and driving away confusion. Keep our minds clear and our harvest fruitful.

LOVE IN ACTION

*Little children, let us not love in word or talk
but in deed and in truth.*
1 JOHN 3:18 ESV

We have been handed an invitation to participate in the kingdom of God. However, it's more than an invitation; it's a mandate expected for every Christian's lifestyle. When God tells us to love our neighbor, our spouses, our children, our enemies, he means more than just verbal confession.

Love is action and not just admission. Christians are to talk and walk in love. When we live in a Christ-honoring, loving manner, it blesses us as well as those around us beginning with our immediate family. Try it. Don't just say it; do it! You will see a dramatic change in your life, your walk with God, your marriage, and your other relationships as well.

Lord, thank you for your Word and revealing to us your purposes and plans. Thank you for involving us in them. We commit to doing more than saying we love you. We will show you with our obedience. To each other, we will not only profess our love, but we will also demonstrate it through our actions.

CALLED OUT

You are a chosen generation, a royal priesthood, a holy nation, His own special people, that you may proclaim the praises of Him who called you out of darkness into His marvelous light.

1 PETER 2:9 NKJV

There is an exceptional difference between a believer's marriage and a worldly marriage. While two people can live together and call it marriage, from God's perspective, there are more requirements. A holy union is something special. It is a calling. What makes sense to God may not seem reasonable to unbelievers and vice versa.

Because a Christian marriage is a calling, it has to be demonstrably different from other kinds of union we see around us. Not only do we reflect the relationship between Christ and the church, but we also create a safe place for family and friends to be nurtured and to grow. We are placed in an essential position within the hierarchy of the church, and we strengthen society by the very structure of a biblically based union. Let us reflect on this calling and do our best to make it as beautiful as our Creator intended it to be.

Lord, thank you for calling us to this marriage. May we demonstrate your calling in our lives by living differently than those in worldly unions. Every day, let us not lose focus of who we are and whom we belong to.

STEP UP

*He was amazed to see that no one intervened to help the oppressed.
So he himself stepped in to save them with his strong arm,
and his justice sustained him.*

ISAIAH 59:16 NLT

Jesus was no stranger to sinners. In fact, he never missed an opportunity to defend the oppressed and forgive the contrite. He did not heed threats or buckle in the face of danger. It didn't matter if his actions were unpopular or stirred up wrath; he was, and still is, committed to justice.

Has God opened your heart to help the disadvantaged? Are you ready to get your hands dirty to help the poor, the lonely, the marginalized, the lost, or the broken? As a couple, how can you step up and intervene on their behalf? If we are to be the hands and feet of God on earth, his chosen ambassadors, let's find ways to get involved. How are you, as a couple, acting as his hands and feet today?

As we consider who we are without your grace, we thank you from the bottom of our hearts for your intervention on our behalf, Lord Jesus. Thank you for dying on the cross for our sins and not leaving us to wallow in our own guilt. Please show us opportunities to intervene on behalf of others and share the good news of your love.

Desire

One thing I ask from the LORD, this only do I seek:
that I may dwell in the house of the LORD all the days of my life,
to gaze on the beauty of the LORD and to seek him in his temple.
PSALM 27:4 NIV

What do you seek? Where is your time spent? Do your desires and pursuits reflect a love for God or a love for the world? Nothing in this world can replace the glory of God. We are inundated daily with empty promises vying for our allegiance, but it is God and God alone who can truly satisfy.

Even our marriages were not meant to satisfy the longing in our hearts for God. We are each blessed with a spouse, and they are a gift from God, but not even they can fill the need we have for our Creator. Everything we encounter has the potential to draw our attention either to or away from God. What draws you to God? Are you actively seeking a relationship with him and fueling the fire within you? Are you encouraging your spouse to seek God, or are you trying to fill their need yourself?

Thank you, almighty God, for satisfying our souls. You made us to need you, and no cheap, knock-off version of happiness can replace the joy we find in you. Help us nurture our relationship as we also encourage each other in the pursuit of you.

GOD FIGHTS FOR YOU

"The LORD your God is the one who goes with you to fight for you against your enemies to give you victory."

DEUTERONOMY 20:4 NIV

What battles are you facing in life? Even in the midst of bleak and difficult times, we have the assurance that we have already won the war. This world and its troubles are temporary, but God's victory is forever, and we are victors with him. Our outcome was decided on the cross, and nothing can steal that away from us.

When the pressures of life weigh us down, when hopelessness creeps into our hearts, or when we feel we have failed, let's be reminded that the Lord God Almighty stands beside us. He fights our battles, and he has already secured our victory.

God, your hand is upon us. You are the shield which protects us from the enemy's deadly blows. Please fill us with strength to face each day's difficulties; we don't have the stamina apart from you. We know that, in you, nothing is too terrible to overcome.

White-Hot

"Because of the increase of wickedness, the love of most will grow cold, but the one who stands firm to the end will be saved."
MATTHEW 24:12-13 NIV

Marriage is a marathon. When we start, our flames of love burn white-hot, but without proper fuel and care, they will dwindle down to embers. Eventually, they will go out and grow cold. How do we keep up the momentum, keep our fires burning, and stay engaged for the long haul?

First, it's vitally important to keep wickedness out of our marriages. Some ills may seem small and trivial, but evil has a way of expanding. Once we invite evil in, it invites all its friends, and it's hard to get rid of once it has made its bed. Second, complacency kills. Fires take work to grow and control. There is no room in marriage for complacency. If we hold on to God and keep loving our spouses more and more, our marriage will stand strong.

In life and our marriage, Lord, please help us keep wickedness out. We want our love to burn white-hot, and we want to stand firm for you.

SHARE THE LOVE

Beloved, if God so loved us,
we also ought to love one another.
1 JOHN 4:11 NASB

God's infinite love is enough to fill our hearts, pour out into our lives, and spill over everyone around us. The basis of love is not feelings or actions; it's experiencing the love of God and witnessing it change us from the inside out.

Just as Jesus offered unconditional love through his life, death, and resurrection, believers are to offer similar love. The love we extend to our spouses, for example, is not given because of how great he or she is but because of how great God is and how he placed us together. Living in love and harmony with one another is an expression of how deep our love and gratitude is for our Father in heaven.

Father God, thank you for the gifts of love and forgiveness. We also thank you for the opportunity of marriage where we can share your great love with each other. You make our marriage strong and delightful. Please teach us to see people through your lens of unconditional love.

ALWAYS SUPPORTED

If I should say, "My foot has slipped,"
Your faithfulness, Lord, will support me.
PSALM 94:18 NASB

The Christian walk is often painted as a precarious existence spent navigating the narrow path. We are warned repeatedly not to mess up, not to make mistakes, not to do this or that, all with the threat of falling away from God or damaging our relationship to him. Yet God does not want us to live a life focused on not doing bad things; he wants us to live a life focused on doing good things. That is what a full existence looks like.

In this passage, the psalmist is celebrating God's faithfulness. He knows that no matter how much he would like to promise it, he cannot guarantee he will not mess up again. He is bound to fail in some way. God, in his faithfulness and commitment to us, knows the same thing. He is willing to support us when our feet slip. When we try to run from him, he will pull us back, and when our circumstances crash, he will be there to support us. Do we have the same grace for our spouses?

God, may we rest assured that on bad days, we will have the faithfulness and commitment to uphold each other just as you uphold us.

ENDURANCE

If we endure, we will also reign with Him;
If we deny Him, He will also deny us.
2 TIMOTHY 2:12 NASB

Marriage, like life, sometimes gets difficult. It can be unpleasant at times, and you might wish to be with someone else or in some other place. In times like these, we need to behave as if our marriage is not about us but rather about our spouses. Marriage is not fifty-fifty. It's better if we each assume that both parties' efforts will be one hundred percent. It's about giving and not taking. However, we are in human relationships which are riddled with potholes and flaws. We need to have the endurance of a long road trip on hard days.

As Paul wrote to Timothy in the verse above, if we endure, we will also reign with Christ in eternity. While this verse focuses on our walk with Christ, it also applies to a God-centered marriage. If we are to honor God as well as our spouses, we will have to endure hard times and awkward situations. The good part is that we come out the other side better than when we entered. The blessing of biblical marriage is a changed, closer relationship with Jesus and with our partners.

Lord, we know that in our walk with you and each other, we will face hardship. We pray that at such times, you will give us the grace to endure and outlast any difficulty. May our relationship be to your glory.

FAMILY

Those who won't care for their relatives,
especially those in their own household,
have denied the true faith.
Such people are worse than unbelievers.

1 TIMOTHY 5:8 NLT

The Lord takes family seriously. He grafted us into his royal family, and he has also given us families here on earth. Regardless of the conflict within your family, we are expected to love and care for them. Relationships take work and sacrifice, but there is a healthy and safe way to follow God's calling to care for those who have also cared for you.

Before we head off to our ministries, work, social circles, or anywhere else, let's make sure we have taken proper care of our families. This begins with your spouse and then extends to children, parents, and other relatives. The Lord has gone to great lengths to care for each of us, his family members, even to the point of his death as an atonement for us. Out of gratitude and love for him, let us take his example to heart and take care of our families too.

Father God, thank you for bringing us into your heavenly family and thank you for our earthly family. Help us love and care for our immediate family as well as our brothers and sisters in Christ.

Life and Peace

The mind set on the flesh is death,
but the mind set on the Spirit is life and peace.
Romans 8:6 NASB

If peace reigns in our hearts, the same peace should be present in our marriages too. How can we profess to putting Christ first in everything if our relationships are not submitted to him?

A dysfunctional and chaotic home life may be indicative of an area not yet under the kingship of the Lord Jesus. After all, the same Spirit who reconciles us to God also works within us and in our relationships. The peace of God brings stability and calm into our hearts, and this carries into our homes. What do we set our minds on? What occupies our thoughts?

God, thank you for the peace with which you flood our minds, marriage, and home. When we become distracted by things of the flesh, please remind us of your greatness and draw us back to you again.

Anger

"In your anger do not sin":
Do not let the sun go down while you are still angry.
Ephesians 4:26 NIV

We can't always help how we feel, but we can help what we do about it. We can choose which feelings to feed and mull over. Regardless of whether our emotions are justified or not, they are how we feel. What can we do when we feel angry? Specifically, what should we do when we feel angry toward our spouses?

This verse does not tell us to not feel angry; it offers two steps on how to handle our anger in a mature, godly way. First, we show self-control by not following up our feelings with acting out. Anger can quickly lead to regrettable decisions if we do not have control of ourselves. Second, we should sort out our feelings and not let them fester. Perhaps a conversation or a walk is needed. Going to bed angry is a great way to lose sleep and wake up even angrier.

Father, please help us maintain self-control when we are angry and sort through our feelings in a timely, calm matter. We never want to sin against you or hurt each other, but we need your help. Thank you.

SACRIFICIAL LOVE

"Since you are precious in My sight,
Since you are honored and I love you,
I will give other people in your place
and other nations in exchange for your life."

ISAIAH 43:4 NASB

God's love is sacrificial. He sacrificed his Son on the cross for us, and it is more difficult for a father to sacrifice his son than it is for him to sacrifice himself. This passage portrays a similar sacrifice. The prophet Isaiah writes that God does not throw away the lives of people as worthless; no one has weighed the cost like he has. He displays his precious favor toward his people and shows them that nothing they have done has landed them in his good graces. They just as easily could have been the "other nations."

That is why God's love and dedication for us is so precious. He loves his people regardless of who they are. Let us not take lightly the understanding that Jesus has called us out of the darkness and into his family.

God, thank you for calling us. Thank you for loving us and making us precious in your sight. May we appreciate your impartial love and the commitment you made to us.

JULY

A man shall leave his father and mother

and hold fast to his wife,

and they shall become one flesh.

GENESIS 2:24 ESV

God's Will on Earth

"Your kingdom come.
Your will be done,
On earth as it is in heaven."
Matthew 6:10 NASB

Does surrendering to God's will require relinquishing all the things that bring you pleasure? Or do you believe you will realize the joy he assured his devoted disciples? In asking for his will to be done, we're not asking for our desires to die but for our hearts to align.

As we live by heaven's ways on earth, our hearts and minds will focus more on what's eternal and what's pleasing to God. We will be less enchanted by the world and its systems. God's will on earth begins with us because that is why he placed us on earth. We would already be in his kingdom with him if we did not have a role to play here and now. What is that role? What is your part in God's will being done on earth?

Almighty God, what is your will? What part do we play? Please align our hearts with yours so we genuinely want what you want.

Limited Vision

Now we see things imperfectly, like puzzling reflections in a mirror, but then we will see everything with perfect clarity. All that I know now is partial and incomplete, but then I will know everything completely, just as God now knows me completely.

1 Corinthians 13:12 NLT

None of us are as smart as we think we are. Time and time again, we realize the way we saw things a year ago was not only inaccurate but perhaps caused us to say things that hurt others. It is Christ's desire that we grow in knowledge and maturity and that we do not allow our perceptions of the world to ignite our anger and frustration hastily.

Our Christian journey is about knowing God better and better as time goes on. There is grace for what we do not know, but let's press deeper into the knowledge of God's character and his creation. God is omnipotent, and he knows his children inside and out. When we finally unite with him in heaven, we will know and perceive like never before.

Lord, give us patience for our loved ones and teach us to seek your knowledge and your perceptions. Nurture us in wisdom as we surrender our lives to you. Thank you for knowing us perfectly.

DO TO OTHERS

"In everything, do to others what you would have them do to you, for this sums up the Law and the Prophets."

MATTHEW 7:12 NIV

The human heart is often hypocritical. We have a double standard when it comes to what we expect to receive and what we are willing to give. Sometimes we don't know we're doing it until someone calls us out on it. It takes mindful and purposeful action to serve others without the expectation of being rewarded. We should form a habit of doing things we would like to be done for us. A few verses before the passage above, Jesus says to remove the plank in your own eye before removing the speck in someone else's; check your own behavior before criticizing another's.

This is particularly important in marriage. Practice offering your spouse what you desire. Take care of their chores for the day, give them an unprompted shoulder rub, or make their favorite dessert. By doing this, you'll learn how to better take care of your spouse and make a habit of assessing your own behavior before judging theirs.

Father, help us lay aside our pride so we may serve each other as you have served us. Make us aware of the opportunities we have to do something special for each other rather than expecting something for ourselves.

RECONCILED

God was in Christ, reconciling the world to himself,
no longer counting people's sins against them.
And he gave us this wonderful message of reconciliation.
2 CORINTHIANS 5:19 NLT

Just as Jesus reconciled us who believe, so we have been entrusted with continuing the work of reconciliation throughout the world. God has given us the responsibility of reconciling with each other, and this includes within our marriages. Our unions are a testimony to the world of Christ's love for his bride, and reconciliation is a core value of marriage since we can't continue on yesterday's goodwill. Each day requires fresh commitment, respect, forgiveness, and love.

If your spouse hurt you yesterday but sincerely apologized and changed their behavior, do not carry that sin into today. We are reconciled to God every day, and he chooses to not remember our past sins.

Your forgiveness is incredible, Lord Jesus, and your reconciliation is perfect. Thank you for your daily grace. May we show daily grace to each other.

THE CREATION OF MARRIAGE

There are three things that amaze me—
no, four things that I don't understand:
how an eagle glides through the sky,
how a snake slithers on a rock,
how a ship navigates the ocean,
how a man loves a woman.

PROVERBS 30:18-19 NLT

The pure love shared within a marriage is one of God's most amazing creations. We learn to love our spouses even more than we love ourselves. We care about them as if they were one body with us. What hurts them hurts us, and we rejoice at their success.

It's impossible to understand and explain the depths of love and loyalty experienced uniquely in this union, but it is by God's design. There is a reason he calls the church his bride; he wants us to understand the depth of his love for us, and that was a picture he knew we could grasp. Of all God's incredible creations, marriage is a beautiful one to behold.

Holy Bridegroom, the way you brought us together, interwove our hearts, and birthed in us a love for each other is indescribable. We praise you, God, for your many wonders but specifically for each other.

Determined to Win

Let us also lay aside every weight, and sin which clings so closely, and let us run with endurance the race that is set before us, looking to Jesus, the founder and perfecter of our faith, who for the joy that was set before him endured the cross, despising the shame, and is seated at the right hand of the throne of God.

Since the Christian life is a race, let us examine the racecourse. We know from the Scriptures how it starts and how it finishes: it starts when we receive Jesus Christ as our Lord and Savior, and it finishes with seeing our hope fulfilled. Between those two points, terrain will be different for each Christian, but we're all headed in the same direction to the same destination.

When we get married, it begins with "I do" and finishes when "at death do us part," but all marriages are going to look different in the middle. The journey is unique for each of us. If we become focused on someone else's marriage or their race with God, it can taint our perspective of our own. We have nobody to compare ourselves to but Christ, so let's keep our eyes forward on him and run our race.

As we race toward you, our worthwhile prize, keep us from distractions like comparison or any other weight which would slow us down and make our journey unnecessarily harder. We have you, Lord, and we have each other. That is enough for us.

SLAVES TO RIGHTEOUSNESS

Thanks be to God, that you who were once slaves of sin have become obedient from the heart to the standard of teaching to which you were committed.

ROMANS 6:17 ESV

Some people have the idea that being married means a loss of freedom. The carnal mind has a different interpretation of freedom than the Christian mind because we already have an underlying mindset that we don't live only for ourselves. This is why we should be careful about what we consume in the media and whom we call friends. These two influences can feed us compelling lies.

Contrary to popular belief, marriage is the freedom to live in a godly way. It is the freedom to experience our strengths and weakness without condemnation and to grow both in serving God and each other. As Paul told the Roman church in the above verse, we have been set free from sin and are now slaves to righteousness. It's a blessing to live for holiness rather than in sin. This lesson is meaningful in marriage because that is where the effects of sin are often the most pronounced. It can bring a lot of destruction, not just to ourselves, but also to the people closest to us as. Thanks be to God that, through Jesus Christ, we have salvation from sin.

Lord, we are grateful to live freely in our marriage through your sacrifice on the cross. Help us always keep you at the center of our lives and our marriage.

God's Counsel

"With God are wisdom and might;
he has counsel and understanding."
Job 12:13 ESV

Life is full of troubles, and we constantly find ourselves needing the advice of others. Perhaps we talk with a counselor or financial advisor or seek wisdom from a parent or trusted friend. If we're smart, we'll ask the opinion of our spouses because two heads are better than one.

Before calling in the professionals, even before going to your spouse, do you seek God's counsel? After all, he holds all wisdom. Yes, we need each other, and we would be foolish not to ask for help when we need it, but let's get in the practice of seeking God first. He has the answer to every problem. Sometimes that answer may come through a person he sends our way. Let's seek him, stay humble, and listen to the wisdom of others because no single person has all the answers.

Father God, we seek your face today. We need your counsel in our life together, and we revel in the mysteries you reveal. You have all knowledge, and we are delighted when you share it with us.

UNITED

Make every effort to keep yourselves united in the Spirit,
binding yourselves together with peace.
EPHESIANS 4:3 NLT

As we walk and grow together as Christian spouses who seek to honor God, we ought to make every effort for each other. Let's pursue peace, exercise patience, and grow in unity and love for each other and for the rest of our spiritual family. The goal of all believers is to develop a Christlike character and demonstrate his love to others.

We ought to pursue peace whenever possible because unity and community matter. A healthy marriage matters. A close family unit matters. All these relationships are important because God is a God of relationships. He wants one with us, and he created us to desire them with others as well.

Father, we want to show others the grace of Christ, the love of the Father, and the fellowship of the Holy Spirit. You have blessed us, and now we want to bless others. Please unite us in your Spirit with your peace.

FAITHFUL TO THE END

"O LORD, you are a great and awesome God! You always fulfill your covenant and keep your promises of unfailing love to those who love you and obey your commands."

DANIEL 9:4 NLT

A marriage is a covenant between two people. This promise also involves God as well as two or three witnesses. Marriage is meant for a lifetime, and the vows reflect this commitment. One of the vital ways believers start the marriage journey is by involving God from the very beginning. God will provide a solid foundation as nothing else can. Just as an insurance policy is intended to protect the value of your belongings from loss, God is the insurance you need for your marriage to make sure it stands the test of time.

The Scripture in today's verse attests to how awesome God is and that he keeps his promises. His covenant with us will last to the end of time for those who keep his commandments. As we commit our marriage lives to him, he will keep his commitment with a steadfast love.

Lord, thank for you for your unfailing love. Your Word stands true no matter what happens in our lives, and we thank you for this covenant with us. We are grateful that our marriage is sanctified and blessed by you.

ENCHANTING LOVE

You have enchanted my heart, my sister, my bride;
You have enchanted my heart with a single glance of your eyes,
With a single strand of your necklace.

SONG OF SOLOMON 4:9 NASB

A Christian marriage is a powerful, beautiful thing. On one hand, marriage represents the love Christ feels for his bride the church. It is a loyal, sacrificial, committed love. On the other hand, since we are all brothers and sisters in Christ, it represents the familial love he has for those who have been grafted into his family by grace.

This brother-sister love is familiar, fun, and safe. Being married, sharing a romantic love and also a shared love for the Father, is unlike any other union on earth. It is, in a word, "enchanting."

We love you, Lord, and we love each other. Thank you for your beautiful creation and masterful design. You have given us so much to be grateful for.

TAKE NO VENGEANCE

"You shall not hate your brother in your heart, but you shall reason frankly with your neighbor, lest you incur sin because of him. You shall not take vengeance or bear a grudge against the sons of your own people, but you shall love your neighbor as yourself: I am the LORD."
LEVITICUS 19:17-18 ESV

Most of us consider vengeance in terms of murder, harm, or some other dramatic action. When God says, "you shall not take vengeance," he follows it up with "or bear a grudge." The two go hand-in-hand. Vengeance does not have to be physical harm. It could be telling someone off or not doing something you know the other person would appreciate. Resentment poisons our actions and words toward people, and that poison is known as vengeance.

Grudges and vengeance go together, and neither of them has a place in a Christian home. Those closest to us often hurt us the most, and it's natural to feel resentment. Acting on it, however, assumes we are worthy of taking vengeance, and that is only for God. That is his role, and vengeance is his. Instead, God requires us to reason with each other in forgiveness and grace.

God, please heal the wounds on our souls today and wash away our grudges and our thirst for vengeance. May we search for your will to be done and for your grace to abound. May we desire your kingdom and not our own.

FULLY COMMITTED

The eyes of the L<small>ORD</small> search the whole earth in order to strengthen those whose hearts are fully committed to him.

2 C<small>HRONICLES</small> 16:9 <small>NLT</small>

The Lord is committed to his people, and he wants this commitment to be returned. He wants a mutually loving relationship with his beloved children. How much does he want it? Today's verse lays out the depth of his desire.

There are no lengths God won't go to save and strengthen those whose hearts belong to him. He loves us so much he will search the entire world and bring us to him by whatever means necessary. Those of us whose hearts are fully committed to him will experience a divine love so unmeasurable and spectacular that all else will pale in comparison.

We are yours, Lord Jesus, fully and forever. Thank you for strengthening us and drawing us to you. We love you and commit to always loving you.

Quick to Listen

Let every person be quick to hear, slow to speak, slow to anger;
for the anger of man does not produce the righteousness of God.
JAMES 1:19-20 ESV

It's easy to open our mouths and hastily respond in the flesh rather than pondering our words and replying in godly wisdom. Do you ever bite your tongue too late and wish you could rewind the conversation? Angry words can damage a relationship in seconds. Misunderstandings and jumping to conclusions can cause us to carelessly lash out and wound deeply.

Relationships need to be carefully and prayerfully protected. In our marriages, where we spend so much time together, it's easy to become angry with our spouses, but this can hurt the deepest because of the love and emotional investment shared. For the sake of our marriages and in response to God's wisdom, let us make sure we are listening, speaking carefully, and choosing righteousness over anger.

Loving Father, thank you for your Word and the wise instructions it contains. Help us be quick to hear, slow to speak, and slow to anger. May we weigh our words carefully with your wisdom so we are mindful of the effects they will have on each other. We want you to be reflected in our speech and our marriage.

BURDENS

Cast your burden on the Lord,
And He shall sustain you;
He shall never permit the righteous to be moved.

PSALM 55:22 NKJV

What burdens are you carrying today? Are worries in your life causing sleepless nights or anxiety? Are you easily set off by your spouse or having a hard time trusting them? You may be shouldering a load you were never meant to carry. The Lord is always nearby and ready to lift what you cannot. It may feel like you're the final defense; surely important things won't get done if you don't do them! But these things are not the problem. Your Father offers unparalleled rest, peace, strength, and endurance so you can do everything you're supposed to.

Are there things in your life you are not supposed to be engaged in? They may be unnecessarily using up your time and energy. Cast them off. Bring them to the Lord. Ask him what he wants you to carry because he is ready and willing to help you.

We can't keep muscling our way through life, Lord, because we grow tired whenever we try. Our strength is not enough. We need you to carry our loads and give us your sweet rest. Thank you for promising to do so.

WEAK BUT WILLING

He gives strength to the weary
and increases the power of the weak.
ISAIAH 40:29 NIV

Do you feel weak and tired today? That's okay. God still wants to give you power and strength. He is not disappointed in you for not having it all together. He is not surprised or disillusioned when you fail or come up short. He is not disgusted by how far below his perfection you fall. After all, he's the one who raises you up. He, and he alone, will give you power, make you strong, help you succeed, and bring you rest. We are not equipped to handle life without him, so rest.

Rest in him. Offer him your broken gifts, your weak faith, and your humble willingness. Offer him yourself in whatever condition you happen to be in today because that's all he is asking of you. Those meager, daily tasks that seem so trivial to us are our simple offering of obedience to him. He can take them and use them for eternal glory. He can accomplish great things through them and through us. Offer him yourself today.

Here we are, Lord, at your feet. Please use us both in our brokenness for your glory and your kingdom. We are weak, but we are willing.

BROKEN YOKE

*Stand fast therefore in the liberty by which Christ has made us free,
and do not be entangled again with a yoke of bondage.*

GALATIANS 5:1 NKJV

If someone bought you a brand-new mansion, would you choose
to live in a tent in the backyard instead? Christ paid a high price
for our freedom. He is preparing the most amazing home for us, so
why would we choose chains? Why would we sit in bondage when
he has given us the key to our freedom?

It may sound ridiculous, but every time we wallow in guilt, every
time we try to earn God's approval through good works, and every
time we scurry back to our old sin, we enslave ourselves again. We
are not enslaved any longer; we are God's children. As such, we
need to stand confidently in our freedom and refuse to let the devil
place his yoke on us.

We know we are not perfect, God, but we are perfectly
loved by you. Thank you for redeeming us and calling
us your children. When we slip back into our old,
enslaving ways, remind us of who we are.

Assurance

*We are confident that he hears us whenever
we ask for anything that pleases him.*
1 John 5:14 nlt

As believers, we believe there are certain things God has taken care of for all time, including forgiveness from sin and eternal life with him. We also know that all things will end up working out for the good of those who love God. Whatever we are involved in, let's keep this perspective and have confident expectancy in our prayers. We know he will answer. We know God hears our cries because we know he loves us. Because we love him, we will ask for what we need according to his will.

Today, let's pray for his will to prevail in our marriages, relationships, careers, and everything else which concerns us. Not only will this grow and mature our relationship with him, but it also realigns our hearts with what is eternally important as we pause to prayerfully consider what we're asking for.

Heavenly Father, we want to walk in spirit and truth, to abide daily in Christ, and to live in unbroken fellowship with you and with each other in marriage. We pray you will grant us these things because we know they are what you desire also.

GIVE

"Give, and it will be given to you: good measure, pressed down, shaken together, and running over will be put into your bosom. For with the same measure that you use, it will be measured back to you."

LUKE 6:38 NKJV

Do you think the Lord does not see when you generously give from your heart? Anyone can give out of their abundance, but when you give out of your need, the Lord is quick to multiply it. Perhaps a friend needed help, and although you were already busy, you stopped to help them anyway. Maybe funds are tight, but you know they're tighter for someone else, and you share what little you have. Have there been times when your spouse needed help or attention when you were tired, but you were there for them anyway?

Here's the truth: you cannot possibly outgive God. He is proud of his children when they're generous because it shows a genuine care for each other, and it proves we trust him to supply for our needs. He will repay us with his heavenly gifts.

Adjust our hearts to be generous, Lord Jesus, because we want to be like you.

A Good Place

Let me hear Your faithfulness in the morning,
For I trust in You;
Teach me the way in which I should walk;
For to You I lift up my soul.
Psalm 143:8 NASB

If we speak about being in a good place, we're happy with our lives, fulfilled in our work, and content in our relationships. Where else would that good place be but in Christ? Considering our marriages, if we are in a good place with our spouses, we are anchored in Christ and being led by him. If a marriage is led by God's Word, prayer, and dedication to his plan, it's in a good place. Even if there are challenges, you can be sure that with your faith in God, you will come out the other side better than when you went in.

As the psalmist wrote in our verse today, we lift up the Lord because of his steadfast love. We can trust in God and therefore husband and wife can trust each other. There is no better place for a marriage than to be centered in Christ.

Lord, we thank you for your goodness to us even though we don't deserve it. You continue to shower us with your love and show us how we should love each other in our marriage. We entrust our lives and everything concerning our marriage to you, dear Father.

Return to the Lord

Let the wicked abandon his way,
And the unrighteous person his thoughts;
And let him return to the Lord,
And He will have compassion on him,
And to our God,
For He will abundantly pardon.

Isaiah 55:7 NASB

The most insidious aspect of sin is how it convinces us we are too far gone to return to righteousness. We look at the red on our ledgers, and we convince ourselves there is no hope; we might as well give up. Perhaps we decide that if we have sinned already, we might as well sin all the more since there is no going back.

There is always an option to go back. Every time we look at the magnitude of our sin, we must remember that the only thing greater is God in his almighty power. Nothing is bigger than God; nothing is stronger. God looks down from heaven at the poor, wretched state of our souls and decides to love us anyway and help us abandon our unrighteous thoughts and ways. If we have the same sense of forgiveness in marriage, a host of resentment, fear, and contempt will be washed away.

Lord, please turn our hearts back to you this day. Teach us to truly appreciate your forgiveness so we can forgive others similarly.

Traveling Blessings

Your wife will be like a fruitful grapevine, flourishing within your home.
Your children will be like vigorous young olive trees as they
sit around your table.
PSALM 128:3 NLT

When you make a decision, do you think about how it will also affect your spouse for better or worse? Do you consider his or her well-being as well as your own? How about the rest of your family, friends, coworkers, and community?

One of the incredible ways the Lord works is through his blessings. They flow further than just you. When you decide to follow and obey God, many other people will be blessed because of you. God is generous, and his blessings multiply. Although our bad actions have consequences that can impact other people, the blessings that accompany our obedience travel much further.

Generous God, thank you for the blessings you give us, our loved ones, and even future generations because of our obedience. You truly are a loving father.

LOVE COVERS

Above all, keep loving one another earnestly,
since love covers a multitude of sins.
1 PETER 4:8 ESV

Love does not treat others critically or mercilessly. If we put down, it means we are also moving downwards. Pulling others up is how we climb. As a society, and especially as a married couple, we rise or fall together. Ridiculing our spouses only hurts the other half of us since we are one: one body, one team, and one in Christ.

Loving our spouse does not mean that we dismiss their sin, but it does mean that we forgive them when they are sorry, we bear with them as they heal, and we remember we also need forgiveness. Christ's love for us covered our sins and washed us clean. This divine love is not blind to faults, but it is gracious and patient.

Dear heavenly Father, thank you for your love which covers our multitude of sins. As you love us while still addressing our sin, teach us how to love each other graciously and patiently. May we speak the truth in love.

GOD'S VIRTUE

*The LORD passed before him and proclaimed,
"The LORD, the LORD, a God merciful and gracious, slow to anger,
and abounding in steadfast love and faithfulness."*

EXODUS 34:6 ESV

In God exists the perfection of all virtue. Think about it this way;
despite his glory, Jesus is humbler than we will ever be. We are
worthless compared to him, yet he will always give himself less
deference than we give ourselves.

Considering this, where is our possibility for pride? God Almighty
himself, appearing in a cloud before Moses, could have given
himself any accolade he wanted, and he chose to identify as the
Lord of mercy, grace, and love. How dare we squabble and elevate
ourselves while God stoops low to be with us? Our only recourse is
to love him and do our best to reflect his character. If he is slow to
anger, let us be the same. If he is abounding in steadfast love, let us
do likewise. It is our privilege to be like him.

How great you are, Lord. You are perfect in every way.
You share your love and humility with us each and
every hour. Thank you for being slow to anger and
abounding in steadfast love so we might encounter
your forgiveness and grace. Please give us the strength
to be steadfast in our love today.

LOVE IN ACTION

"I was hungry and you gave me something to eat, I was thirsty and you gave me something to drink, I was a stranger and you invited me in…. Truly I tell you, whatever you did for one of the least of these brothers and sisters of mine, you did for me."

MATTHEW 25:35, 40 NIV

Love recognizes the needs of others and seeks to address those needs. Sentiment is perfected through action. God, in his abounding love, did not sit idle while we were in sin but sent his Son to us. In the same way, God wants us to show our love for those around us by giving food to the hungry, water to the thirsty, and a place of belonging to the estranged. The difficulty is that it can be uncomfortable, and we are often as blind to the needs of our closest people as we are to strangers' needs.

Most people treat strangers more courteously than their own children and spouse, but we need to remember that "the least of these" might just be sharing our bed. Perhaps he or she is the one from whom we are withholding our generosity. We should seek to love each other through our actions rather than just our words.

Lord, you are endlessly generous. You give constantly. When there is need, you provide answers to the humbled. Oh God, give us hearts like yours that see struggle and seek to share that difficulty to alleviate it as best we can.

SOWING AND REAPING

Do not be deceived: God cannot be mocked. A man reaps what he sows. Whoever sows to please their flesh, from the flesh will reap destruction; whoever sows to please the Spirit, from the Spirit will reap eternal life.

GALATIANS 6:7-8 NIV

Although God can supersede any natural law, he fashioned them with a purpose, and he usually allows them to run their course. Basic logic maintains that whatever effort we put into something, we will see similar results. By that reasoning, what we put into our marriage will directly correlate with what we get out of it.

Do you take your spouse for granted, or do you treat them like the gift from God that they are? You can't withdraw more than you deposit. The crop we harvest has everything to do with the seeds we plant long beforehand. God's natural law of cause and effect applies to marriage the same way it does to anything else. Don't be deceived; it's worth adhering to.

Heavenly Father, develop generous hearts in us so what we say and do brings honor to you and strength to our marriage. We will take the time to sow your good seeds, dear God.

AUTHORITY OF SCRIPTURE

All Scripture is God-breathed and is useful for teaching, rebuking, correcting and training in righteousness, so that the servant of God may be thoroughly equipped for every good work.
2 TIMOTHY 3:16-17 NIV

It is no surprise that the Word of God is useful for many things necessary in a Christian's life; it was given by God's inspiration. It unveils his holy character and unfolds before us his divine plan for mankind. It convicts us of our need for a savior and teaches us about our involvement in God's plan. It informs us what God expects of his children and guides us along the road of righteous living.

It trains us how to walk the path of patient endurance, and it furnishes us with examples of lives of humble obedience. It is an indispensable part of any godly marriage, a critical element for building an unshakable foundation, and it sustains spouses committed to God and each other for the long haul.

Thank you, loving Father, for your inspired Scriptures. Teach us, convict us, correct us, and train us through your living, powerful Word so we may be equipped to carry out the work you have ordained for us in marriage and ministry.

COMPASSION AND GRACE

You, Lord, are a compassionate and gracious God,
slow to anger, abounding in love and faithfulness.
PSALM 86:15 NIV

One of the most delineating hallmarks of a mature believer is how much grace they extend to others. It's difficult in any relationship, especially a marriage, to show love through mercy and grace. Over time, it can be hard to handle even the smallest annoyances and offenses created by your spouse.

The Bible tells us that God is full of compassion and grace. He is slow to anger and steadfast in love and faithfulness. He does not treat us the way we deserve. As believers in Christian marriage, we can extend that same grace, compassion, and steadfast love we have received from God. We want to bless our spouses with the best we can give since we have been given the best by our Lord and Savior. We do not have the luxury of holding grudges or nursing hurts when compassion and grace have been poured out on us.

Lord, your Word says you are compassionate and gracious. You are our patient, loving, and faithful God. This is also our calling. Please open our hearts, Father, and give us your Spirit to enable us to extend grace, love, and compassion to each other.

COMFORT EACH OTHER

Comfort each other and edify one another,
just as you also are doing.
1 THESSALONIANS 5:11 NKJV

Does the prospect of spending eternity with Jesus motivate you to encourage and edify others? Instead of becoming dismayed as world's chaos unfolds, remind one another of the better day which lies ahead. As Christians, we look forward to the day when Jesus returns and all wrong is made right. In the meantime, let us help one another in our walks with Christ so we may all be better equipped to serve Him.

In looking for others to comfort and edify, the perfect place to start is with your spouse. Marriage is a constant opportunity to encourage each other toward Christ because a strong union between a husband and wife can accomplish amazing things for the kingdom of God.

Lord, the hope you give us is both assured and eternal, and that provides us with incredible comfort. Regardless of how grim things may appear, you bring light and encouragement. Similarly, we want to offer your light and encouragement to others. We want our marriage to be edifying and comforting. We know that we are stronger together.

Fulfilling the Law

Love does no wrong to a neighbor;
therefore love is the fulfillment of the Law.
Romans 13:10 NASB

We may be familiar with the maxim that a person can kill two birds with one stone. We are not in the business of killing birds, but it just means that a person is achieving more than one thing with the same action. Romans 13:10 tells us that love does not harm a neighbor; love is actually the fulfillment of the law.

In the Old Testament, the law was emphasized in the lives of the Israelites, so it became more about the rules. Thanks to God's perfect plan, however, when Jesus came as a man to be the sacrifice for our sin, he simplified things. Loving your neighbor is fulfilling the law. Marriage is not about fulfilling burdensome requirements, intricate legalities, or endless rules. It is simply about love. Just love your spouse and you are on the right track.

Lord, thank you for the new covenant in Jesus Christ that frees us from legalistic life. Thank you for the love you have given freely to us. May we love each other with intention.

DEADWEIGHT

Jesus said to him, "Let the dead bury their own dead,
but you go and preach the kingdom of God."
LUKE 9:60 NKJV

Things that are deadweight take up time, effort, and resources. These are precious commodities and shouldn't be spent on anything that isn't a blessing to God or others. Sometimes the deadweight seems really important, and we believe we must attend to it. But upon closer examination, we realize it is a waste of our time, energy, resources, or all three.

If we carefully and prayerfully consider what should take up space in a marriage, the results will be edifying for us and God. Maybe there is a place with an activity for you and your spouse or a job that will build the relationship. When Jesus gave the above reply to the man who wanted to be his disciple, he wasn't belittling the importance of burial rights or the grieving family; he was explaining the higher priority of following him. It's important that we focus on what is eternal and not allow the deadweight of this temporal world to drag us down.

As we live in this world, it's easy to become distracted with things vying for our attention. We want our attention to remain on you, Father God. Please give us the wisdom to recognize what is actually important and what is dragging us down.

AUGUST

An enemy might defeat one person,

but two people together

can defend themselves;

a rope that is woven of three strings

is hard to break.

ECCLESIASTES 4:12 NCV

GIVE AN ACCOUNT

Each of us will give an account of himself to God.
ROMANS 14:12 ESV

Our spouses will not give an account for us to God. Neither will our parents, our pastors, or our bosses. Only we, and God, know what's in our hearts. Are there areas he has asked you to surrender that you are struggling to release? From the outside, it may look like you are living a godly, righteous life, and you may even be able to fool your spouse, but you can't fool God. Each one of us will stand before him and answer for our lives.

The thing about surrendering to God is that it always works out better for us. It may feel like we have to let something go, but what he gives us in return outranks anything he asked us to surrender. If you still feel you can't let go, well, here's more good news; God wants to help with that too. Just talk with him. Answer for your actions now instead of waiting until the end of your life. It's worth it.

Please help us, loving Father. We want to fully surrender every area of our hearts to you, but we need your strength and courage to do so.

LOVE AND HATE

Let those who love the LORD hate evil,
for he guards the lives of his faithful ones
and delivers them from the hand of the wicked.

PSALM 97:10 NIV

Hatred is an emotion created by God. It was not born out of hell but born out of heaven as a response to hell. If God is to be truly holy, his spirit must be in accordance with all things good and reject, unequivocally, all things evil. That is what hatred should be: rejection of true evil.

Unfortunately, we often use hate as a rejection of anything that does not please or satisfy us. We hate things wrongfully so often that we have forgotten what is proper to hate. According to the psalmist, "Those who love the Lord hate evil, for he guards the lives of his faithful ones." Our love of the Lord, our faithfulness to him, and our hatred of evil are all bound together in one life of commitment. Faithfulness, hatred, and love also play an important role in marriage. We must hate the things that threaten it but also love and display faithfulness to our partners.

God, give us the right kind of hate. Teach us to stop using hate for our own purposes and teach us to wield it, along with love, for what is right.

YOUR BEST

Whatever you do, do your work heartily,
as for the Lord and not for people.
COLOSSIANS 3:23 NASB

If you had to go to a significant job interview or a meeting with an important person, you would want to present yourself in the best possible light. This same attitude should be displayed in a marriage by both husband and wife. While we are married to human beings who are inevitably sinners, we are still fulfilling a divine calling. Such a calling from an almighty God encourages us to serve fully and not with halfhearted conviction.

Colossians 3:23 emphasizes the need to work with a positive, fully engaged attitude and with a need to please God rather than people with our work. We should have this attitude in marriage as well as in life. When your day requires you to love your spouse, serve them, or work to provide for them, may it be done with a heart submissive to the Lord.

Father God, let us not be complacent in the way we serve you or each other. Help us always serve as if we are doing it for you and not simply for a person. Thank you for the example of Christ who did not compromise in his calling on earth.

UNDIVIDED DEVOTION

I say this for your own benefit, not to lay any restraint upon you, but to promote good order and to secure your undivided devotion to the Lord.

1 CORINTHIANS 7:35 ESV

What others may see as a restraint, lovers of God view as an honor and a privilege. We know devotion to the Lord and upholding his laws do more for us than for him. The Lord gave us laws for our benefit; they "promote good order" and help us live the best lives possible, and that is what God wants for us.

God knows that what we need most is him. He needs nothing, but he wants us. We need him. Undivided devotion will result in a deeper relationship with him, more satisfaction in life and in our marriages, and a better understanding of our calling and purpose which leads to fulfillment. If anyone has misled you into believing that Christianity is just a bunch of rules meant to stifle our excitement, you can rest assured that nobody is more exciting than the Creator himself, and he has big plans for us.

We offer you our undivided devotion, dear Lord. We rejoice in your laws and thank you for the benefit they bring to our lives.

A NOBLE WIFE

An excellent wife is the crown of her husband,
but she who brings shame is like rottenness in his bones.
PROVERBS 12:4 ESV

To be noble means to possess excellent morals and character. Our verse today speaks of the blessing of a noble wife to her husband but also of the burden a shameful wife is to him. In simple terms, a wife's character reflects upon her husband in a good way or a bad way. This verse is easily flipped; husbands reflect on their wives too.

A good character is like a crown, and a bad character is like bone rot. Those are powerful images! Crowns bestow high value upon the wearer and entail a high status. It shows how much value a spouse can bring to their partner or how much value they can take away. It all depends on their character.

Lord, thank you for the blessing of marriage and for your Word which gives a clear perspective on what a godly marriage looks like. Good character and morals come from you, imparting to us the high value that brings blessing to ourselves, our spouses, and you.

WALK IN LOVE

*Walk in love, just as Christ also loved you and gave Himself up for us,
an offering and a sacrifice to God as a fragrant aroma.*

EPHESIANS 5:2 NASB

In this verse, Paul says to walk in love. He says this is right because
Christ loved us and gave himself for us. He did this not out of selfish
desire, gain, or as a return on an investment but as "an offering and
a sacrifice." This love, as brutally and violently displayed as it was on
the cross, is a fragrant aroma to God. It is the truest form of love, for
it is perfected in unasked-for generosity. It is a love Jesus walked,
lived, and died in. This is the love we are to walk in.

When you look at your spouse, do you see someone you are willing to
give yourself up for? Do you see someone you are willing to not just
rely on and be relied upon but someone you are willing to lose your
very life for? When you look to gain nothing in return, that is love.

Oh God, make our lives a sacrifice and a fragrant aroma
to you. May the way we treat others, especially each
other, be righteous actions of love that display your
kingdom on earth.

SACRIFICIAL LIVING

I have been crucified with Christ; it is no longer I who live, but Christ lives in me; and the life which I now live in the flesh I live by faith in the Son of God, who loved me and gave Himself for me.
GALATIANS 2:20 NKJV

Self-preservation is strong among humans; it is why self-centeredness comes naturally to most people. If you are married or looking forward to getting married, however, that is a habit you will need to address. Marriage has a way of showing us our selfish side.

Galatians 2:20 tells us that Paul was crucified with Christ so his sinful, self-serving side would perish, and he could be a new creation. This attitude prevails in strong, healthy marriages, and it enables us to serve each other and glorify God. We need God's wise Spirit to do such a magnificent self-check and be new creatures every day.

Lord, thank you for your Word as Paul spoke to the Galatian church. This epistle helps us live by faith and glorify the Son of God by crucifying the flesh. Help us follow Christ's example in our lives and our marriage so we may be stronger and more selfless every day.

DO NOT WORRY

Refrain from anger and turn from wrath;
do not fret—it leads only to evil.
For those who are evil will be destroyed,
but those who hope in the LORD will inherit the land.

PSALM 37:8-9 NIV

God does not take acts of evil lightly. What is evil? Anything that goes against God. That is why worrying leads to evil; it reveals a lack of trust in the Lord. As Christians, we have a source of strength, given to us by God, which the world cannot attain. Therefore, we should not be acting like the people of the world who act without hope.

Instead of worrying, let's hope in the Lord. He has a perfect track record of faithfulness which predates our existence, so it is not misplaced hope. Do not fret and expose your lack of trust. Are you worried about your marriage, or do you trust your spouse? Are you worried about your future, or do you trust your Father?

Worry is so blinding, God. Please give us peace and help us see things as they are. We are not of this world, and we do not dabble in the anxiety of this world. Our hope is in you, dear Lord. You are faithful and true, and we know, without a doubt, that you will take care of us.

EXERCISING FAITH

Prepare your minds for action and exercise self-control.
Put all your hope in the gracious salvation that will come to you
when Jesus Christ is revealed to the world.
1 PETER 1:13 NLT

Those who regard Christianity as a crutch or believe faith is a cop-out have never tried to live it. Faith in Christ is active and living. There's no sleeping on the job when it comes to faith. It is not reactive or passive. Putting all our hope in someone requires two virtues which aren't required quickly or half-heartedly: trust and confidence. Faith will require our entire minds, hearts, and lives. It requires self-control and trust.

Like exercise, faith is easier when you can share it with someone who can walk beside you and keep you moving forward. Have you ever gone on a run with someone, and it spurred you on to try harder and go farther? It's the same way with faith and hope, and that's why it's invaluable to have a spouse ready to run life's race beside you.

Victorious God, we know you are right beside us as we run this race. Thank you for this partnership you have given us so we can encourage each other along.

TREASURE YOUR SPOUSE

How beautiful is your love, my sister, my bride!
How much sweeter is your love than wine,
And the fragrance of your oils
Than that of all kinds of balsam oils!

SONG OF SOLOMON 4:10 NASB

Do you place your relationship with your spouse higher than all other relationships apart from with God? Do you give him or her higher importance than all comforts and frills of this world? Marriage is a special gift from God, and it's important that we treat it like the valuable blessing that it is. Your spouse is God's beloved child whom he entrusted to you. Do you delight in your spouse? Do you listen to them, learn from them, strive for the best for them, and keep them on the top of your priority list?

True to God's nature to reward obedience, we will quickly realize that when we delight in our spouse, we will find them more exciting and satisfying than all the luxuries of this world. Truly treasure the partner God has blessed you with.

Heavenly Father, you have filled this earth with wonderful things, but greater than all the sunsets, cuisines, friendships, and luxuries is the enjoyment you give us through each other. We are so grateful. May we always take care of and treasure one another.

LOVE AS LAW

The whole law is fulfilled in one word:
"You shall love your neighbor as yourself."
GALATIANS 5:14 ESV

The Old Testament law is massive in its breadth and depth. Scribes and theologians have spent millennia plumbing its depths and finding joy in its intricacy. For Paul to say that "the whole law is fulfilled in one word" is a huge statement, yet it also makes sense considering the heart of God.

The whole law is inspired by the Creator who desires to be near his people even though they are separated from him by their sin. Everything that separates them is evil born out of selfish desire, pride, or other things that do not accord with the Spirit of God. The opposite to all these things is love, born out of a true and whole heart that seeks the Father's will. We fulfill the law through love because that is the end goal of the entire law. The same principle is lived out within marriage. There are many tips and strategies to a healthy marriage, but they can all be summed up by this: love your spouse as yourself.

God, teach us to fulfill the law by caring for our neighbors and each other as we care for ourselves.

FRUIT OF LOVE

Hatred stirs up strife,
But love covers all offenses.
PROVERBS 10:12 NASB

Every tree bears its fruit. This biblical truth is found mostly in the gospels, but it's also here in Proverbs. The writer speaks of the different results, or fruits, of love and hate. Just as we learn later that love fulfills the whole law, here we learn that love covers "all offenses." We can prescribe temporary solutions for the divisions in our relationships, but it is the hard labor of love that will heal them.

If apathy is the lack of love, hatred is the opposite of love. It is a force with the opposite goal but the same amount of energy and emotional investment. Rather than fixing issues, it creates them. It seeks to hurt someone, so they know how we feel. It seeks destruction to release us from our own personal, emotional bondage. But hate does not work. It is unwilling to cause its own destruction. By feeding it, we make it grow. We stir up more strife and succumb to a new master.

Lord, work in our hearts this day to fight our anger with your love. Please be opposed to it and cover our host of offenses with it.

LOVE AND RESPECT

Each one of you also must love his wife as he loves himself,
and the wife must respect her husband.
EPHESIANS 5:33 NIV

The love a man is expected to have for his wife, and the respect a woman is expected to have for her husband, are both a lot to demand. Paul says "let" as if it were that easy. For a husband to love his wife as himself means to live with her flaws as he lives with his own, to push her as he pushes himself yet not out of hatred, and to care for her as if her body were his own.

For a wife to respect her husband almost demands more because it requires her to trust him and the decisions he might make. Love and respect are not easy to build, but they are the foundation of marriage, and both parties need both virtues.

Dear Jesus, we need you every hour. Help us deny ourselves in love and respect for each other. We need you because we cannot carry out this soul-changing work without your grace and strength.

TWO WORLDS

By faith Moses, when he became of age, refused to be called the son of Pharaoh's daughter, choosing rather to suffer affliction with the people of God than to enjoy the passing pleasures of sin, esteeming the reproach of Christ greater riches than the treasures in Egypt; for he looked to the reward.

HEBREWS 11:24-26 NKJV

Moses stood between two worlds: the unbelievable wealth and luxury of the pharaoh's palace and the slavery of the Hebrew people. Yet Moses understood that the real decision was between the fleeting fortunes of this perishing world or the richness of a loving relationship with his Creator, Yahweh. When you have eyes for eternity, the decision becomes quite simple, and yet it's still so hard.

The world we live in is full of the glorification of sin and the worship of self. It offers so much instant gratification that it's difficult to remember to keep looking forward. Remember, when moments of decision crop up throughout life, keep eternity in view.

Nothing in this world compares to knowing you, Lord God! We want a loving relationship with you more than anything else.

GOD'S STRENGTH

My flesh and my heart may fail,
but God is the strength of my heart
and my portion forever.
PSALM 73:26 NIV

The way we live betrays what is in our hearts. When we believe that God has put his Spirit in us, we walk with more confidence and less worry. Instead of concerning ourselves with the small portion we've been temporarily given, we eagerly anticipate our forever portion with God our Father. On earth, our bodies will eventually decay, but our eternal lives are hidden with Christ.

There is a strength placed in us which is stronger than our flesh and hearts. We can't physically or emotionally match it, yet it is in us because God has plans for us that far surpass what we could accomplish on our own. Let's live knowing this and not allow our flesh or hearts to hold back God's strength within us.

Oh God, please use us for your glory. We submit our bodies and hearts to you, and we believe you have put your strength in us for your eternal purposes.

Love and Faithfulness

"Yes, I have loved you with an everlasting love;
Therefore with lovingkindness I have drawn you."
JEREMIAH 31:3 NKJV

Have you ever considered how God's love for us lasts longer than our existence? His thoughts of us, his considerations and plans, and his desire for our salvation all predate us and will carry on with us into eternity. The love we have for our life partners should be the same. Years before we have seen their faces, we should be praying for them and thinking of their place in our lives. When we meet them, love can flourish and give glory to God through its beauty. If they die, that love can continue as a thankfulness for the time God gave.

This is the source of faithfulness. It is the child of love, a deep and personal love, transcending emotion and choosing to put someone else's well-being above our own.

Precious Savior, reveal your love to us and make us the people we struggle to be. Forgive us of our many sins so we might love you wholeheartedly. Let the love we have for you fuel the love we have for each other.

PRAYER IS PURPOSEFUL

*Pray for us, too, that God will give us many opportunities
to speak about his mysterious plan concerning Christ.
That is why I am here in chains.*
COLOSSIANS 4:3 NLT

A marriage between believers is grounded by prayer, but saying a prayer and living a life of prayer are different. If we don't want to be surprised by the enemy's attack, we need to be watchful and give attention to our spiritual well-being just like a guard at a city gate. In practical terms, this means prayer was not intended to be a careless, casual, or frivolous act. Prayer is a purposeful conversation with our Creator. Our enemy wishes to destroy us, our marriages, and anything designed to bring glory to God.

If there is chaos and division in your marriage, or if Christ is not being glorified through it, the devil may have you in spiritual chains. The greatest way of escape is through prayer. After all, what could be more bonding than praying together regularly?

God, thank you for letting us come directly to you through prayer. Chains or no chains, you are always close by and ready to help us. We want you to be the center of our marriage, and we ask you for opportunities to share the good news of Christ even if that's simply through encouraging each other as partners in Christ.

LIVING BY FAITH

*By faith Abraham obeyed when he was called to go out
to a place that he was to receive as an inheritance.
And he went out, not knowing where he was going.*

HEBREWS 11:8 ESV

Living by faith is easier said than done. It's easier imagined than lived. It's a grand adventure, but it can also be nerve-wracking and uncomfortable. God is jealous for your heart, so he will always be on a quest to draw you closer to himself and thus further away from any comfort which threatens his place in your heart.

True faith requires trusting God's Word more than the wisdom of the world. Living by faith means believing God's promises are true and expecting them. Faith obeys even if the path hasn't been made clear, just as Abraham obeyed when he left his homeland even though he didn't know where he was going. Like Abraham, we were saved by faith, called out of the world, credited with God's righteousness, and promised an inheritance.

Father God, we don't often know where you're leading us, but we know you, and that's enough. We want to live by faith, so help us find our comfort, hope, and home in you and not the world.

Spirit of Power

God has not given us a spirit of fear,
but of power and of love and of a sound mind.
2 Timothy 1:7 NKJV

Spirits of fear are commonplace. Spirits of anger are easy to find. Paul's declaration is that we have neither of these spirits in Christ but instead a spirit of power, love, and a sound mind. These traits are beyond human ability to attain. It is only by the grace of God that any human has the capacity to live with these virtues. The power Paul speaks of is not like the fake shows of power we are used to here on earth. Paul's power is the almighty power of God poured into his saints through the Holy Spirit. It is a quiet but unstoppable power. That is the spirit of power that animates our being.

The love in this passage is a deep, all-embracing love. It is a love easily hurt by injustice and evil but strong enough to endure every hurt. The sound mind Paul speaks of is a weapon, a disciplined, trained, rational mind that we control by God's might rather than letting it control us.

God, give us this day a spirit of power and love. This day restore our minds to us as sound, strong minds. Make us weapons of your making.

SERVING GOD

If you suffer for doing good and you endure it, this is commendable before God. To this you were called, because Christ suffered for you, leaving you an example, that you should follow in his steps.

1 PETER 2:20-21 NIV

We all feel taken advantage of at times and even by our beloved spouses. Maybe you don't feel properly appreciated for all you do. When these feelings creep in, remember that a godly marriage is not about what you can get out of it but what you can give to God through it.

Perhaps a conversation needs to happen between you and your spouse, but the more important matter is that you recognize you serve God through your marriage. Living in this world is difficult, but if you're suffering because you're serving, remember how commendable this is before God. Remember intimately the example Christ gave you so you would have the wherewithal to endure.

Dear Lord, we serve you by serving others, and often we suffer because this life is hard. When we feel discouraged or underappreciated, please remind us that you see us. We endure for you. Thank you for the example you gave through your own life and thank you for calling us to you. Even when it's tough, you're worth it.

INNER BEING

I pray that out of his glorious riches he may strengthen you with power through his Spirit in your inner being, so that Christ may dwell in your hearts through faith.

EPHESIANS 3:16-17 NIV

God does not lack resources. We spend our lives working and earning money to provide for our families and loved ones, but this is not the case with God. He has glorious riches, and from his great wealth, he strengthens us with power through his Spirit. That Spirit resides in our very souls. It is not a superficial coat of paint that changes our appearance but a deep, transformative Spirit who has penetrated and soaked into who we are on an irreversible level.

This relationship, this presence in our inner being, is only cemented through faith. Faith is a form of trust, and that trust manifests itself through our actions when we seek to grow in oneness with God. Faith is also a commitment. It's a day-to-day process where we die to ourselves and choose to put Christ forward and seek him rather than other things that try to get in the way.

Dear Christ, give us the strength to have faith, and make that faith a catalyst for us to grow closer in oneness to you. Similarly, give us the faith to be committed to each other as partners, and make that commitment a way for us to lean into each other.

RESPECT AND PURITY

Wives, be subject to your own husbands, so that even if some do not obey the word, they may be won without a word by the conduct of their wives, when they see your respectful and pure conduct.

1 PETER 3:1-2 ESV

Little do we know what power respect and purity have. Actions speak louder than words, and respect may be more persuasive than a debate. If we can talk someone into something, someone else smarter may be able to talk them out of it. But strength of character to this level cannot be earned by emerging triumphant from a battle of wits; it's only through a steadfast commitment to trust and follow the Lord.

If you are married to an unbeliever, or you have a close friend or family member who has not given their lives to Jesus Christ, the best thing you can do is respect them and keep your actions pure, so your life stands as the testimony.

Father, we're coming before you today to pray for (name of loved one). We ask you to work in their life and use us as a testimony of your forgiveness. Please give us the wisdom to know when to respectfully speak and when to remain quiet for our actions do the talking. Thank you, God, for who you are and everything you do.

LOVE'S PASSION

Set me as a seal upon your heart, as a seal upon your arm,
for love is strong as death, jealousy is fierce as the grave.
Its flashes are flashes of fire, the very flame of the LORD.

SONG OF SOLOMON 8:6 ESV

God paired love with passion to give it strength to accomplish great things. Love is a fierce, formidable force not to be taken lightly. It has great power and can cause severe damage as "the very flame of the Lord." Yet from this fire can also come warmth, new life, and vitality. To say "love is strong as death" is a bold statement. Death is one of the few absolutes common to all humankind, and its finality is relentless. Yet the relentless nature of death is what the writer chooses to compare love to as other analogies fall short of the scope and breadth of love's power.

God is love. God is omnipotent and mighty, full of quick-acting passion and deep suffering. His jealousy truly is "fierce as the grave," and his dedication and love for us is even more relentless and assured as death itself.

Oh Lord, your love is power. Your love is like fire. Give us the same love for one another and most of all for you so our lives may be passionate and not apathetic.

GOD'S EYES ONLY

"Beware of practicing your righteousness before other people in order to be seen by them, for then you will have no reward from your Father who is in heaven."

MATTHEW 6:1 ESV

There's a quiet peace and confidence that comes from the process of learning true integrity when good works flow from our honest love for the Lord rather than the desire to impress others. The Lord judges by the heart and not by outward appearance as we do. He's not watching for how many times we stop and help an old lady across the street. He's not keeping a tally of the good things we do. He's looking at the way we think about him and others.

This can be a terrifying thought. We know we are sinful. We don't always dwell on what is pure and lovely, but we can have peace in the knowledge that Jesus died for those impure motivations, and he is sanctifying us in this life until the day he comes back.

Lord, you are fully righteous. You know when our hearts aren't motivated by what is good. Please convict us of any hypocrisy in our lives; help us reflect you both in our inward hearts and our outward actions. Work through our weaknesses to display your perfection.

GOD IS LOVE

We have come to know and have believed the love which God has for us. God is love, and the one who remains in love remains in God, and God remains in him.

1 JOHN 4:16 NASB

"God is love" encapsulates his very essence. The love of God touches every corner of our hearts and reaches into every aspect of our lives. When our marriages become a monotonous humdrum and our daily lives feel empty, God's love is there, ready to reignite our fire. Behind the black clouds of sin shines the Son of redeeming love. Waiting patiently beneath the dreary fog of hopelessness sits our loving provider.

If you are falling out of love with life, your spouse, your calling, or whatever else, consider that you may be falling out of line with God. God is love; the two cannot be separated. Are you filled with love? Are you full of God? The capacity you have for love is a direct correlation of how much you have filled yourself with God's goodness. Spend time in prayer, mull over his Scriptures, think on his goodness and greatness. Familiarize yourself with this powerful love God wants to give you and truly believe it.

Oh God, you are love! We want to remain in you and your love. When we feel our love depleting, we will come running back to you so you can fill us up again.

Born of God

Beloved, let's love one another;
for love is from God, and everyone who loves
has been born of God and knows God.
1 John 4:7 NASB

We tend to look like our parents because of genetics, and we act like our parents because of their influence in our lives. Since God the Creator is our Father, as the idea which became us was birthed in his mind, we look like him. The more time we spend with him, following his guidance and learning from his ways, the more we act like him.

As we understand his immense love, we in turn become more loving. God is love, and there is no separating one from the other. Therefore, if we are truly his children, we will also have an immense love for others. God's love flows to us, through us, and out to others. There's no way to contain it because it is who he is, and it becomes who we are as we grow more like him. Love is what identifies us with God.

Loving Father, we want to grow more like you. We want to love others the way you do, so help us first recognize and accept the incredible love you have for us.

Unconditional

"Love your enemies, and do good, and lend, expecting nothing in return, and your reward will be great, and you will be sons of the Most High, for he is kind to the ungrateful and the evil."
Luke 6:35 esv

We are only capable of loving our enemies by the power of Christ. He loved us while we were still his enemies, so he knows the kind of strength we need to love those who have wronged us. There are moments when we feel vitriol and hatred instead of the love we know Jesus expects of us. Those moments, big or small, are opportunities to fall on the mercies of God.

Failure is certain when we rely on any human strength to forgive. Only God has the infinite stores of love and self-control we require. He is willing to give them to us but only when we ask him and repent of our own pride. In this heart posture, God can make us "kind to the ungrateful and the evil." In this posture we give more glory to God than we will know for a long time.

God, give us the love for our enemies that identifies us as your children. Help us love unconditionally just as you loved us and to extend mercy to those who do us wrong.

Abraham's Faith

No unbelief made him waver concerning the promise of God,
but he grew strong in his faith as he gave glory to God,
fully convinced that God was able to do what he had promised.
ROMANS 4:20-21 ESV

This passage is speaking of the righteousness counted to Abraham because of his faith. The blessing he received was granted to him not because of all the good things he did in his life but because of his faith in the Lord. When tested on the mountain, Abraham even had faith that God could raise his son from the dead. He knew without a doubt that what God says, God does.

These verses should challenge us. We can assess ourselves and ask if we are living in a faith that believes God's words are true. The one who spoke the universe into existence is worthy of our trust. We know from Scripture that God wants what is best for us, and what is best for us is an intimate relationship with him. There will be times when he doesn't do exactly what we want him to do, but our job is to trust that he is in control in every circumstance.

God, when we put our faith in ourselves instead of you, remind us of Abraham. Please show us that you are working all things for the good of those who love you.

WITH ALL

Jesus said to him, "'You shall love the Lord your God with all your heart, with all your soul, and with all your mind.'"
MATTHEW 22:37 NKJV

There is no commitment like the commitment that gives its all. Anyone who harbors an area of their life untouched by the love of God falls short of Christ's standard. That means we all fall short. We are to love the Lord because he is our God. As the personal God of our hearts, we are to love him with all we have and in every area of our lives. We are to give him all the emotional outpouring of our inner being, exalting him through the heart's total commitment.

Similarly, we are to love him entirely with our souls and minds. If our hearts are in a place of piety but our minds are darkened by temptation or enmity, God's love is not perfected in us. It must penetrate into our waking and subconscious thoughts. This commitment to love God is the source of our commitment and love within a relationship.

Oh God in heaven, enrapture our spirits and enfold our minds. Saturate us in awe so we may love you with all that we are and commit tirelessly to your exaltation. Make this the posture of our hearts, minds, and souls.

WHOLESOME TALK

Let no unwholesome word come out of your mouth, but if there is any good word for edification according to the need of the moment, say that, so that it will give grace to those who hear.

EPHESIANS 4:29 NASB

As humans, we talk all the time, and in marriage, both the content and the context of talk is essential. A person can get to the point in marriage when there is very little talking, or what is said is not edifying to God or the marriage.

Especially in marriage context, how we talk has big implications; it's the difference between joy and resentment. Sometimes a word you did not mean to say escapes, and it then must be addressed at that moment to prevent further damage from occurring. Remember that words can build up or break down a relationship. Speak your words carefully so you do not grieve the Holy Spirit as you talk.

Lord Jesus, thank you for your Word. We are grateful that your Word guides our speech as well as our deeds. We pray that your Spirit will guide our words and thoughts. Let us always have grace as we talk with each other in this marriage.

CHRIST WITHIN

Him we proclaim, warning everyone and teaching everyone with all wisdom, that we may present everyone mature in Christ. For this I toil, struggling with all his energy that he powerfully works within me.
COLOSSIANS 1:28-29 ESV

When Jesus Christ takes up residence in our hearts, he brings new desires, principles, motives, and goals with him. His transforming presence reshapes us and, suddenly, our lives take on new meaning. He becomes the source of power for our marriages, jobs, ambitions, ministries, and friendships. We become shining lights on a hill for all who are lost in darkness to see.

A Christ-centered marriage, for instance, is a powerful force for good in a world where self-seeking reigns supreme. Christ replaces our pain and brokenness with love, fulfillment, and purpose.

Lord, you brought the two of us together and united us through marriage. When we center our marriage around you, it thrives and grows. Not only is this a blessing to us, but it also gives us a stronger foundation to help serve those around us and be a positive force for good. Thank you for healing our hurts when nothing and no one else could.

SEPTEMBER

Don't owe anything to anyone,

except your outstanding debt

to continually love one another,

for the one who learns to love has

fulfilled every requirement of the law.

ROMANS 13:8 TPT

Loving When It's Tough

*"I say to you, love your enemies
and pray for those who persecute you."*
Matthew 5:44 NASB

The challenging point in this passage is how we are commanded to love when it is the least natural and least desirable course of action. Loving our enemies and praying for those who persecute us is not as easy as cursing them and pushing on with the energy of contempt. God does not promise to help us if we build up resentment; he promises to help us build up love.

The situation is similar in marriage. When your spouse is mean to you, even to the point of purposeful cruelty, praying for them is still God's path. Your actions must be inspired by love and the desire to bring your spouse back to God in every moment. Our actions have to be guided by prayer, so rage and self-exaltation do not consume us. This is the difficult life God has set before us.

Lord, you love us with unconditional love. You love us with a never-ending love guided and inspired by a desire to care for us. Please fill us with this same love and help us love our enemies enough to pray for them earnestly.

LOVE'S VALUE

*If I speak in the tongues of men or of angels, but do not have love,
I am only a resounding gong or a clanging cymbal.*

1 CORINTHIANS 13:1 NIV

God has great power and magnificence. He can do anything, and he has often made displays of his mighty arm at work to prove this. He also has great wisdom, and no mortal mind can plumb the depths or reach the breadth of his thoughts. Yet these things are not what the apostle Paul reveres in this chapter of 1 Corinthians. Rather than "speak in the tongues of men or of angels," he would have love.

Further on, he puts love above strength, the powers of prophecy, and even the sacrificing of one's own life and belongings. Having any of these things, or doing any good work, without love is of no value in Paul's eyes, and neither should it in ours. Speech without love reduces it to just sound. Any action without love, most notably in our marriages, will not take hold or have affect. Our commitment to our spouses has to be paired with a commitment to act in the sincerest love we can.

God, bring color to our actions and lives through your love. Fill us up, Lord, so we may pour over into those around us.

OUR HELPER

We can confidently say, "The Lord is my helper;
I will not fear; what can man do to me?"
HEBREWS 13:6 ESV

When we are following God, we know that all is going to come together for good no matter what. If we make a mistake, God can help us correct it, and he makes a way for us through it. He helps us even when we don't deserve it—because we never deserve it! He already paid for our sins and mistakes. What better reason do we have to help our spouses and extend the same grace?

It is not our job to judge our spouses; that job is way above our paygrade. Sure, some issues need to be addressed for the sake of a healthy marriage, but our job is to love and care for our spouses, to help them when they need it, and to show them grace because we've been shown grace.

Our confidence comes from you, dear Jesus. There is nothing that your blood cannot deliver us from. Thank you for helping us when we are truly helpless. In turn, we promise to help each other and be gracious.

Be the Example

Let no one despise you for your youth,
but set the believers an example in speech,
in conduct, in love, in faith, in purity.
1 Timothy 4:12 ESV

Paul gave Timothy a list of character traits that every Christian spends their life seeking to attain and grow. Speech, conduct, love, faith, and purity are at the heart of ethical Christian living, and marriage is no exception. It takes love to bring two separate people into a unified existence and to learn to accept the other's weakness and humanness. It takes faith to center a marriage on Christ rather than each other and to grow in Christian devotion. Finally, purity provides marriage with a safe space to flourish and grow.

When we practice these three virtues in our marriage, it becomes a mature marriage that no one will despise. It makes the marriage an honorable example rather than a warning to others.

God, grow our marriage in maturity. Let it mature into an image of love, faith, and purity. Grow our marriage in holiness and admirability.

COMMITTED TO THE LORD

*"May your hearts be fully committed to the Lord our God,
to live by his decrees and obey his commands, as at this time."*

1 KINGS 8:61 NIV

The most important aspect of Christian marriages is that we commit to the marriage, to each other, and to God. It is a powerful trifecta of commitment with God at the center. It flows between the husband, the wife, and God. As we read in 1 Kings 8:61, "And may your hearts be fully committed to the Lord our God, to live by his decrees and obey his commands, as at this time."

This verse is the last statement from the benediction of Solomon to God when he dedicated the new temple. The whole of Israel was in attendance as Solomon urged everyone to recommit to God. It was a massive ceremony with huge numbers of animals sacrificed and a week-long feast for all attendees. It was a ceremony of commitment much like a wedding is. The Israelites publicly stated their faith in God and committed to walking in his ways. Marriage is also a commitment to God and to walking in his ways. God wants us to understand his Word establishes his marriage as the blessing between two people who are committed to him and to each other.

Lord, thank you for giving us your Word, your Spirit, and your guidance. Keep us committed to you and to your Word. May we follow your ways in everything we think, say, and do.

SCALABLE VIRTUE

"Whoever can be trusted with very little can also be trusted with much, and whoever is dishonest with very little will also be dishonest with much. So if you have not been trustworthy in handling worldly wealth, who will trust you with true riches?"

LUKE 16:10-11 NIV

The world of what-ifs is a world of lies. We can't know for certain what we would have done in other circumstances. We can't know anything for sure if it has not already happened. This world of what-ifs is the world we fall into when considering how much more virtuous we would be in other circumstances. If our jobs were better, if our spouses were better, or if our struggles were just of a different variety—not medical, social, or something else—then we would be great people. Then people would see our true selves.

God did not put us into the circumstances we have idealized. He has put us here, in this moment, to live the life of his choosing. He put us here for a reason. Our job is to live this life the best we can rather than wish for another life. We follow his voice, and wherever we land, we trust it is for God's ultimate glory, and we do our best. This is a life well lived.

God, please nurture our appreciation for the spouse you have given us in each other. May we grow to appreciate their beauty rather than yearn for something different.

GOOD WORKS

"Let your light so shine before men,
that they may see your good works
and glorify your Father in heaven."
MATTHEW 5:16 NKJV

The point of good works is not to earn salvation or convince others that being a Christian means we don't do bad things. We do good works because we are grateful to God for the salvation he has already given us. We also do good works so others can see the change God has performed in our lives. It is for the glory of God that we do good works.

This is immediately applicable in marriage because sometimes we do good things for our spouses without the reciprocity we were hoping for. Still, we continue to love and serve them because of our gratefulness to God. Marriage isn't about what you can get out of it, and it's rarely fair. If your motive is to love God by loving your spouse, and you're letting your good works shine like a light, there's a good chance your spouse is praising and glorifying God in their heart. Others will take notice of the powerful marriage you have too.

The point of it all is you, God. Our lives, our marriage, and our good works are all a testimony to how great and powerful you are. May we shine brightly for you.

STAYING FOCUSED

*The one who looks into the perfect law, the law of liberty,
and perseveres, being no hearer who forgets but a doer who acts,
he will be blessed in his doing.*
JAMES 1:25 ESV

The black storm clouds of life and the tumultuous waves of discontent are designed to shipwreck our testimony and set us adrift from the anchor of our soul. In those moments, when it is easier to look around and become frightened, anxious, or overwhelmed, James encourages us to keep our eyes on Jesus.

One of the ways believers go astray is by forgetting what we have been taught. We become careless in our Christian walk and drift away from the narrow pathway to life. Losing focus on God means we lose focus on everything God has called us to including our marriages. It is one thing to hear God's Word and a whole other thing to hide it in our hearts and put it into practice. Today, let's look into his Word and remember what it says by practically applying it to our lives.

Heavenly Father, thank you for this reminder to keep our eyes fixed on Jesus and our hearts focused on the truth of your Word. Thank you for freeing us from the curse of the law of sin and death; help us follow the law of the Spirit of life in Christ Jesus.

SALVATION

By grace you have been saved through faith.
And this is not your own doing; it is the gift of God.
EPHESIANS 2:8 ESV

Salvation is a gift. Furthermore, it is a gift only God can provide. Regardless of how desperately we want to grant salvation to another person, we can't. It doesn't matter how hard we try to earn it on our own; we are unable to. Forgiveness of sins and eternal life is given by God alone. Our task is not to save people or earn our way to grace. We are called to share the good news of the gospel, be living examples of it, pray for the salvation of others, and help people grow in the grace of God. We were created for good works, and we have been saved to serve Christ.

Yes, we were created for something far more glorious than the world could offer or imagine. Intrinsically crafted by God, each of us has an important role to play. When we get married, two carefully crafted individuals are knit together along with their dreams, desires, strengths, and abilities. How does your marriage reflect your role in the kingdom of God?

Nothing you do in our lives is by mistake or coincidence, Father God. Your plan is perfect, and your Word is true. Thank you for saving us when we did not deserve it and for giving us a role to play in your kingdom.

LOVE OTHERS

If I had the gift of prophecy, and if I understood all of God's secret plans and possessed all knowledge, and if I had such faith that I could move mountains, but didn't love others, I would be nothing.

1 CORINTHIANS 13:2 NLT

What would your marriage be without love? What if your spouse served you, did everything you asked, and brought you presents, but didn't love you or care about getting to know you? Would you be happy in a relationship like that?

Imagine how God feels. He doesn't just want our obedience and our sacrifices, and he isn't impressed with our grand gestures of good works. God loves us, and he wants us to love him. He asks us to love him by loving others. It makes sense that we start by loving those he has placed closest to us like our spouses and families. Everything we do means nothing if it's not out of and for love.

Lord, please teach us how to love you by loving others even better every day instead of trying to fulfill some moral checklist. We love you.

NOT BLIND FAITH

Faith is the certainty of things hoped for, a proof of things not seen.
For by it the people of old gained approval.
HEBREWS 11:1-2 NASB

The Almighty has a flawless track record of perfect judgment and keeping his promises. Our hope in his Word is not wishful thinking or betting on the most likely outcome. Our hope is assured because God always does what he says he will do. Our faith is certain even though we cannot see the outcome.

The confidence we have in the Lord is not "blind faith," as some would accuse it of being, because even though we cannot know the future, we can know God. He has proven since the beginning of time that he is trustworthy, so we don't need to stumble around blindly. He wants to be known, and he has earned our complete trust. That is how we know our future with him is certain.

Thank you, God, for not requiring a blind faith from us but instead proving time and time again that you are faithful. We can place our hope confidently in you.

SUPPLEMENTED WITH LOVE

For this very reason, make every effort to supplement your faith with virtue, and virtue with knowledge, and knowledge with self-control, and self-control with steadfastness, and steadfastness with godliness, and godliness with brotherly affection, and brotherly affection with love.

2 PETER 1:5-7 ESV

Peter says to "make every effort." That is a lot to demand of someone. That is a whole-person commitment of mind, soul, and body that focuses our entire existence onto a goal, but it is worth it. Faith without virtue will give someone the label of Christianity but not the clean reputation our Lord deserves. Virtue without knowledge is unprotected and vulnerable, and knowledge without self-control can be cruel. Beyond all these things, Peter places love as the fundamental supplement. It is at the heart of human interaction between intimate partners, those passing on the street, and members of a congregation. We are to season all our interactions and our faith with love.

The Bible is not exaggerating when it says that God is love, and Peter knows it. In between our faith and love stands virtue, knowledge, self-control, steadfastness, godliness, and brotherly affection. These are similarly not to be neglected in our Christian walk, but the bookends holding them together are faith and love as two key pillars of a Christian life.

God, work in us to perfect our faith with awe in your love. Make this marriage a team of virtue and love.

RENEWED MINDS

Do not conform to the pattern of this world, but be transformed by the renewing of your mind. Then you will be able to test and approve what God's will is—his good, pleasing and perfect will.

ROMANS 12:2 NIV

There is the way the world operates, and there is the counter-cultural way believers operate. We are different because our motivation is different. Pay attention to the slogans companies use to peddle their products, and you'll hear an array of self-pleasing jargon appealing to buyers' desires for instant gratification.

As Christians, we live for a greater kingdom and God's everlasting rewards. Our lives, by default, become an example of an alternate way of living. It may not make sense to people of the world, but their minds have not been renewed by submission to the Lord. With our minds renewed, we're able to know what God's will is because we're more attuned to him than we are to what is around us.

Oh God, we deeply desire to know what your good, pleasing, and perfect will is. Please continue to renew our minds and reshape our lives. We know we will seem different to others, even confusing, but we live for you and you alone.

TESTS OF FAITH

The LORD your God led you all the way these forty years in the wilderness, to humble you and test you, to know what was in your heart, whether you would keep His commandments or not.

DEUTERONOMY 8:2 NKJV

During our time on earth, we encounter hardship and heartbreak. For those who aren't living for eternity, difficulties are just plain difficult. For those of us who hope in the Lord, trials can be tests of faith which make us stronger. They are opportunities to express our love for Christ, act on our commitment to his Word, and be a testimony to those who haven't seen the light of God's love yet.

As we walk through trials and tribulations, let's remember that our hope is not in vain. Our faith in the Lord is well placed.

Heavenly Father, we are grateful for life, good health, peace, and joy. We thank you for each other, our family, and our friends. God, please teach us to be thankful for challenges we are confronted with; you may be using them to mature us and prepare us for what lies ahead.

GOOD GIFTS

Every good and perfect gift is from above,
coming down from the Father of the heavenly lights,
who does not change like shifting shadows.
JAMES 1:17 NIV

Marriage is a good and perfect gift. Of course, it's filled with imperfect moments because it is between two flawed individuals, but marriage itself is perfect because it is an institution God set up to reflect his love for his bride. What we do within our union either to disgrace or uphold that image is up to us.

The Lord gives good gifts. It is in our best interest to receive them gratefully, use them carefully, and be faithful to share them with others. If you are grateful for your spouse because you know they were given to you by God, chances are you will be careful to uphold and protect your marriage. If you do this, chances are your marriage will be full of love. How can you share that love by blessing others as a couple?

Unchanging God, you are not shifty like the shadows of love this world offers. Your gift of love is forever. Thank you for this marriage. May it be full of love, and may we have opportunities to bless others because of it.

ALL THINGS

I can do all this through him
who gives me strength.
PHILIPPIANS 4:13 NIV

What would you attempt for God if you knew you would not fail? If you truly believed you could do all things because of his strength at work in you, what things has God placed on your heart to do? What do you desire to use your God-given strength for? What does your spouse have on his or her heart to do? What strengths does he or she have? When you combine your desires, callings, and strengths together, what do you think God may be calling you to as a couple?

There is nothing the Lord calls you to that he does not also equip you for. He might not give you everything you need all at once but take a step forward in faith. Watch him pave the way.

Oh Lord, please keep us from settling. Please awaken our hearts to what you are calling us to and strengthen us to walk your calling. Thank you for this marriage. Use us to strengthen and refine each other.

BETTER TOGETHER

If one person falls, the other can reach out and help. But someone who falls alone is in real trouble. Likewise, two people lying close together can keep each other warm. But how can one be warm alone?

ECCLESIASTES 4:10-11 NLT

Any predator knows that the easiest target is a lone target. That's why animals often travel in herds and why God created us to be part of a community. We are made to be in fellowship and to have families and friends. Marriage is a beautiful way to have a close friend, an accountability partner, and even stay a little warmer at night.

We long for companionship because we were created in God's likeness, and he longs for companionship. Nothing and no one can fill the void we have in our hearts for him. However, he also designed us to want relationships with others which bring us both joy and greater protection. We're simply better together.

Lord God, thank you for this marriage and the special bond we share. Thank you for the loving family and friends you have placed around us and for perfectly designing us to be communal.

ENTRUSTED TO GOD

Commit your work to the LORD,
and your plans will be established.
PROVERBS 16:3 ESV

Like everything else we entrust to God as believers, it's important we give control of our marriages fully to the Father. As believers, we seek to have God control all areas of our lives, and we cannot minimize how important our marriages are when we trust in him.

Proverbs 16:3 puts it perfectly. According to the Merriam-Webster dictionary, one of the meanings of "establish" is something that is growing or flourishing successfully. Success means different things to different people, but a truly successful marriage can only come from being established and rooted in God and in his Word. Reading Scripture and following the Word encourages us and allows us to establish our marriages and our lives in Christ. The Scriptures give us direction and stability to renew our support for each other every single day.

Lord, thank you for your love and grace and for giving us order in an otherwise chaotic world. Lord, help our marriage be established in you and in your Word. In you is everything good and worthy.

BLUEPRINTS

Commit everything you do to the LORD.
Trust him, and he will help you.
PSALM 37:5 NLT

If we are going to do something or go somewhere, we need some guidance, a plan, or a map. If we are making a building, we need blueprints for the house. The blueprint of marriage is found in the Scriptures. Following God's path for marriage results in a strong and resilient structure for the family to flourish.

Psalm 37:5 tells us to commit our way to the Lord. What a blessing it is to know that we don't have to figure things out by ourselves! We don't have to grope in the dark or experiment with what works and what won't work because the Bible is our guide to all life and to marriage in particular. Everything we do, say, or think needs to be in line with God's Word because it is the true guide.

Lord, thank you for being our guide on the path of life. We depend on your leading and your Spirit as we walk the marriage journey. Let us always depend on you and trust you every step of the way.

FORSAKING ALL

*"Whoever of you does not forsake all that he has
cannot be My disciple."*

LUKE 14:33 NKJV

Did God ever take something away from you and then replace
it with something better? Perhaps you had a crush on someone
before you ended up with your spouse. Maybe you were rejected
for a job or school, and your life went in a different direction.

Whatever your story, the story of God remains the same: his way is
the best way. Sometimes God closes a door, but other times he asks
you to close it. He wants to know if you trust him. Is he asking you
to lay something down today? Perhaps it's something bad he wants
to dig out of your life. Maybe it's something good that he wants to
replace with something better. In the end, if all we have is Christ,
we have more than enough.

For you, Lord, we forsake all. If there is anything in our
lives that we're clinging too closely to, that's impeding
us from fully following you, please help us surrender
it. There is nothing we want more than to be your
disciples and follow your example.

FAITH DEFENDS

In all circumstances take up the shield of faith,
with which you can extinguish all the flaming darts of the evil one.
EPHESIANS 6:16 ESV

We can't fight a spiritual enemy by natural means. Our greatest enemy, death, was already defeated by Christ on the cross on our account. By faith in his resurrection, we too have victory over death. Still, the enemy knows our weakest points, and he aims his fiery darts at the bullseye of our human frailty. He will use fractured relationships, money concerns, health issues, and other concerns to tempt us to focus on our problems and take our eyes off Jesus.

May we be more astute than that! Always remember that anything which may cause our hearts to fail can be overcome when we bring all our cares to Jesus by faith. Faith is our shield and best defense.

Heavenly Father, thank you for fully equipping us to overcome the world, the flesh, and the devil with powerful, spiritual armor. Please help us stand fast in faith on your promises and to keep our eyes on Jesus rather than our problems.

POWER OF PATIENCE

Wait for the LORD;
Be strong and let your heart take courage;
Yes, wait for the LORD.
PSALM 27:14 NASB

Look around. Do you see a world of patient, self-controlled people who are content with life and confident in who they are? No, we see a population of discontented, disgruntled individuals who struggle with their self-worth and always seem to be in a frantic hurry.

There is an overarching strength and courage found only in time spent with the Lord. There is peace and assurance only discovered while waiting, watching, and experiencing the work of God firsthand. We exert so much energy into trying to put our life together, impress God, and get on to the next best thing, but God wants us to sit with him for a while. He wants to walk the journey with us and show us a better path. Let's take some time today to seek him and patiently prioritize listening to what he has to say. In doing so, we will find all the strength and courage we need.

We need your strength and courage, Lord God. We need you every moment whether we remember it or not. Instead of running around frantic like worldly people, we want to take your hand and deliberately walk down a better path with you.

MOTIVES MATTER

Am I now seeking the approval of man, or of God?
Or am I trying to please man?
If I were still trying to please man,
I would not be a servant of Christ.

GALATIANS 1:10 ESV

Has anyone ever called you a "people pleaser"? If so, it probably didn't sit well. There is nothing wrong with pleasing people. In fact, the Bible is clear about our mandate to love, serve, and care about others. The difference, however, is your motivation.

Motives matter because God cares about your heart. If our efforts to please people are simply to garnish favor or approval, that is not an adequate motivation because we have already been approved by the Lord. His opinion is the highest, most qualified one. If we serve others because we love God and he has filled our hearts so full of love that we are driven, as children of God, to serve, that is a purer motive. We serve people because we serve Christ.

When we consider what motivates us to wake up in the morning and work hard all day, we want it to be because it pleases you, dear God. Help us keep our motives pure.

DAY AND NIGHT

The LORD will send His goodness in the daytime;
And His song will be with me in the night,
A prayer to the God of my life.

PSALM 42:8 NASB

There are times when the sunlight of God's love is blotted out by the clouds of life. Just because we cannot see the sun does not mean it isn't there. Our appreciation and desire for the love of God is designed to deepen through the dark times of our lives. That is why the psalmist's posture is one of hope and resilience. He hopes for the goodness of God and know that it will come eventually in the "daytime."

The psalmist is also aware of his current emotional state and that his soul is cast down within him. With that in mind, he prepares and comforts himself with a song of the Lord that "will be with me in the night." This "prayer to the God of my life" is recognition from the psalmist that it is God, and not him, who holds his life.

Oh Lord, give us faith to weather the dark times of this life. Give us a song to sing in the darkness and a hope for the morning.

Paradox

"Whoever exalts himself will be humbled,
and whoever humbles himself will be exalted."

MATTHEW 23:12 ESV

God's kingdom does not work the way our world works. Here, if you humble yourself at work, the promotion will probably go to someone else. If you humble yourself in an argument, the contender will probably walk all over you. Nothing gets past God, though, because our merciful Father is also a just king. He raises up and lowers down people at his perfect discretion.

With this in mind, which kingdom does your marriage model? Do you insist on your own, stake your claim, hold your ground, and keep records of rights and wrongs? Or do you put your spouse first, listen and then talk after, and humble yourself for them? It may seem paradoxical, but God's ways always end up being the best ways.

Father and King, rather than learn from the systems of this world, we want our marriage and lives to follow the structure of your kingdom. The more we learn about you, the less the world impresses us.

EXTENDING GOD'S LOVE

"By this everyone will know that you are my disciples,
if you love one another."

JOHN 13:35 NIV

What is the difference between a believer and an unbeliever? What is the difference between a believer's marriage and an unbeliever's marriage? The key difference is in what they love. Although two unbelievers may sacrifice for each other, the marriage is by nature self-seeking; it was based on two individuals seeking what was best for themselves and finding pleasure in each other.

When two believers who want to please the Lord find each other and fall in love, the basis for their union is how they can better serve the Lord together. Their first and most clear witness of God's love to the world now becomes how they love and treat each other. That is what anyone on the outside will see first. Is the basis for the marriage self-interest, or does it exist in and for a love which is greater than either of them?

As believers, we recognize that we reflect you to the rest of the world, and the world learns of you by how we love each other. Although we often stumble, Father God, we want everything we do in our marriage to exemplify the love you have shown us. Please fill us and our marriage with mercy, kindness, compassion, sympathy, and care that overflows. May others want to know you more as a result.

RUN TO GOD

"Fear not, for I am with you;
be not dismayed, for I am your God;
I will strengthen you, I will help you,
I will uphold you with my righteous right hand."

ISAIAH 41:10 ESV

We all have fears, but God, in his righteousness, protects us from sin and death. Evil is everywhere, but we need not dismay at the condition of the world because God upholds us. It doesn't matter what hurdles are standing in our way because God is already preparing a way through them. When we sin, God forgives us and helps us when we are contrite and go to him.

Adam and Eve were so ashamed of their sin that they tried to hide from God, but God is a just and loving father whom we ought to run to and not away from. His righteousness saves us and not our own. Let us remember the grace God has shown us and extend that grace to each other. When we mess up, let us run to God for the help he is willing and ready to offer.

Help us, dear Father, to run to you when we need help. You strengthen, uphold, and protect us from the evil that threatens to destroy us. You teach us how to have grace on ourselves and on each other.

FOSTERING COMMUNION

All the believers devoted themselves to the apostles' teaching,
and to fellowship, and to sharing in meals
(including the Lord's Supper), and to prayer.
ACTS 2:42 NLT

We form habits, some good and some bad, in our lifetimes. We want to cultivate good habits especially in marriage. One good habit is having meals together and catching up on the day. Another good habit is spending time in the Word together and sharing perspectives on how the Word spoke to you. Yet another habit worth embracing is to enjoy fun things together like books, movies, or exercise. Whatever it is, cultivating an activity that involves both of you goes a long way in fostering strong ties.

Acts 2:42 discusses some shared activities amongst the early believers. These brought people together and strengthened the bonds they shared as believers and as family. The same principles apply in marriage. If our marriages are to grow and be strong, communion and regular fellowship must be ingrained in the fabric of our shared lives. This is how our marriages can be healthy, strong, and edifying to the Lord.

Lord, thank you for the example of the early church we find in the Word. Thank you for the relationships they formed with each other. May we use the same techniques our own Christian walks and marriage.

THE LORD'S WILL

Come now, you who say, "Today or tomorrow we will go to such and such a city, spend a year there, buy and sell, and make a profit"; whereas you do not know what will happen tomorrow. For what is your life? It is even a vapor that appears for a little time and then vanishes away. Instead you ought to say, "If the Lord wills, we shall live and do this or that."

JAMES 4:13-15 NKJV

Is your life exactly how you thought it would be? Did you marry the person you thought you'd marry or have the exact number of children you predicted? Is your career what you thought it would be? Do you live in the house of your dreams? Probably not all of those things, right? Only God knows the future, the best we can do is make flexible plans.

Life throws everyone curveballs: some exciting, some tough, and some devastating. The way we face disappointment can grow our faith faster than almost anything else. We want good things in life, but God wants the best for us. Even when we don't understand, we can know that everything he does is out of his perfect love for us.

Whatever your will is, Lord, that is what we want. When we don't want what you have designed, please soften our hearts, open our minds, and continue to have grace on us while we learn. Thank you for all you have given us and everything you have withheld. Your way is best.

The Seventh Virtue

As God's chosen people, holy and dearly loved, clothe yourselves with compassion, kindness, humility, gentleness and patience. Bear with each other and forgive one another if any of you has a grievance against someone. Forgive as the Lord forgave you. And over all these virtues put on love, which binds them all together in perfect unity.

Colossians 3:12-14 NIV

At the heart of the gospel are six central qualities each of us should possess: compassion, kindness, humility, gentleness, patience, and forgiveness. However, there is one above them all. Love is the highest virtue.

Love is the greatest because, when we truly possess love, all other virtues follow naturally and more easily. Love binds them all together and identifies us as children of God. We can forgive because God forgave us. We can love because God loves us. This is the gospel message.

We love each other, Lord, because you loved us first. We can forgive each other because you have forgiven us. May these virtues be ever-present in our marriage as a testimony of our love for you.

OCTOBER

Love is large and incredibly patient.
Love is gentle and consistently kind to
all. It refuses to be jealous when blessing
comes to someone else. Love does not
brag about one's achievements nor
inflate its own importance.

1 CORINTHIANS 13:4 TPT

COMPASSIONATE JUSTICE

"This is what the LORD of armies has said: 'Dispense true justice and practice kindness and compassion each to his brother.'"
ZECHARIAH 7:9 NASB

What does it mean to dispense true justice? How do justice and compassion go together? In order for one of these attributes to be perfectly practiced, it needs the other. As a culture, we tend to tolerate all sorts of behavior in the name of kindness. If we become so fixated on being kind that we lose sight of right and wrong, we become passive participants in the perpetuation of sin. On the other hand, if we get so caught up in advocating for justice that we stop listening, stop caring, and stop having compassion, we miss the point, and God is not glorified through our actions.

True justice cares about others and lovingly, patiently insists on what is right. The place we start showing justice and compassion first is in our own homes with those closes to us: our "brothers."

Teach us, Lord, to show justice, kindness, and compassion the way you do. Please help us never separate them, and may our efforts be effective and pleasing to you.

ACTS OF LOVE

*If I give all I possess to the poor and give over my body to hardship
that I may boast, but do not have love, I gain nothing.*

1 CORINTHIANS 13:3 NIV

It is not enough to do the law; we must embody the law. That is
only possible by the heart-changing work of the Holy Spirit who
works to produce the fruit of the Spirit within us. The Bible says that
love covers a multitude of offenses and fulfills the law, and we see
that played out in this verse from 1 Corinthians. Even when Paul
goes above and beyond in his works by giving away all he has, it
counts for nothing. Paul must have the spiritual presence of love in
his soul, a love that only God can create, if he is to "gain" anything.

It is similar in marriage. The gifts we give, the service we render,
and the things we say will fall on deaf ears if they are done with a
heart of stone. In the midst of our commitment there must be life,
sincerity, and a passion only possible through the Holy Spirit.

God, impassion our hearts with your spirit and love.
Make us able to do the works of your will.

BECOMING ONE

*This explains why a man leaves his father and mother
and is joined to his wife, and the two are united into one.*
GENESIS 2:24 NLT

The commitment of marriage is one of utter dedication in mind, body, and spirit. This passage emphasizes the body. When two are joined in marriage, there is a change that takes place in the authority of the flesh. 1 Corinthians 7 discusses this change by explaining that the wife's body belongs to her husband and the husband's to his wife. When we marry, we take on a responsibility for the bodies of our spouses. We are no longer independent beings who suffer alone, rejoice alone, and make our own way. It requires tenderness and vulnerability to entrust our bodies to our spouses.

The Bible frequently compares the bodily dedication in marriage to God's desire for spiritual unification with his church. Marriage doesn't mean living in the same house with someone you like; it means openness and willingness to share your deepest hurts, insecurities, and dreams with someone you trust to listen. It also means being ready to listen when your spouse is vulnerable with you.

Father, thank you for the gift of marriage. Teach us to forsake our pride and individuality so we might discover a new and better identity in our union together. Please help us trust each other with our minds, bodies, and spirits, and to do our part to be worthy of that trust.

Unmerited Devotion

This is real love—not that we loved God, but that he loved us and sent his Son as a sacrifice to take away our sins.

1 JOHN 4:10 NLT

Our devotion to God is a response. We are not faced with an unloving God whom we choose to love anyway. We are caught in amazement by a God who loves us while we do not deserve it. The point John is making here is that true love is not a reaction to love received. It is spontaneous, unmerited, and full of grace for another's mistakes and sins. God's love is truer than ours because ours will always be an outpouring of the love we receive.

There is no shame in this. When we choose to love those who are harsh with us, when we give respect to the disrespectful, we pour out the love of God. We display the nature of God's heart to those who might not see it otherwise. In a relationship, we should be the first to extend an olive branch, the first to give grace and forgive, and the first to love. This is the nature of God's response to our sinful and wretched state.

Dear Lord, thank you for loving us while we were still sinners. Thank you for giving yourself when we had turned our backs to you. Thank you for seeking us when we wanted to do nothing but run from you. May that love overflow to other people we meet.

LOVE MOTIVE

Love does not delight in evil but rejoices with the truth. It always protects, always trusts, always hopes, always perseveres.
1 CORINTHIANS 13:6-7 NIV

What does real, Christlike love look like in action? These verses offer a beautiful description. Love defends the character of the other person as much as possible within the limits of truth. Love won't lie about weaknesses, but neither will it deliberately expose and shame them in other people. Love believes a person is innocent until proven guilty and offers them the benefit of the doubt.

If there is a problem, love takes ownership and doesn't immediately blame the other person. It is not pessimistic. It anticipates success for their loved ones, not failure, and sacrifices for their success. Love cheers, "I know you can do it because God is able!" Love does not ignore reality or close its eyes to problems, but it rests on the promises of God.

Lord, thank you for showing us what real love looks like. We pray for this kind of love in our marriage and in our other relationships as well. Please empower us to love like you do.

THE FIRST RELATIONSHIP

God created human beings in his own image. In the image of God he created them; male and female he created them. Then God blessed them and said, "Be fruitful and multiply. Fill the earth and govern it."
GENESIS 1:27-28 NLT

The very first relationship God created amongst humans was a perfect partnership between a man and a woman. He knew they were better together, and he created them to perfectly complement each other.

Another important realization is that we are made in God's likeness because God also wants relationships with us. He is relational and deeply desires to share his love with us. Coming together in marriage is only a reflection of the love God feels for us. He is so overflowing with love that he has filled us with it and filled our lives with other people to love.

Mighty and wonderful God, you have so much love to give. Thank you for creating us to be the recipients. Thank you for the gift of relationships and for blessing us with the family and friends you have placed in our lives.

THE GREATEST

Faith, hope, and love remain, these three;
but the greatest of these is love.
1 CORINTHIANS 13:13 NASB

God is a god of omnipotence, omniscience, and omnipresence. He is unfathomable in every way, and his mind and heart know no end. Humans are tiny in comparison. Our thoughts are not of eternal value. The legacy we leave on this planet is comparable to a drop in the ocean of humanity's history. Out of all the facets of human existence, there are three aspects of us that do last beyond our existence: faith, hope, and love.

The faith we have in God brings us into eternal relationship with him. The hope we have in Christ and share with those around us has unending value. The way we live by love, fulfilling the law through love and following God's commands out of love, is the greatest of these three eternal virtues. None of us can reach the level of humility Christ had, but we must put every effort toward love. Of everything that will last, love is the greatest.

Lord Jesus, remind us what has merit and what does not. Teach us to invest in things that remain forever.

ENDURING FOREVER

Give thanks to the LORD, for he is good;
his love endures forever.

1 CHRONICLES 16:34 NIV

We are like dust in the wind, swayed easily by emotions and outside forces. A single comment can plant a seed of rage in us that lasts for days even while we pray against it and seek God's peace. Humans are weak, and nothing about us is reliable. We can rejoice and be glad that God was not made in our image because if he were, his love would not endure forever. He would not be good all the time. His love would not be steadfast or withstand every unfaithful and hurtful thing we do against him.

No, our God is good and faithful because of the ways he is unlike us. We should seek to mimic God's steadfast love. Because of how important our spouses are to us, anything they do can anger us. These are the moments we should endure with steadfast love by pushing into the character of God.

Lord in heaven, you are eternal, and we are a moment. Let us use this moment of ours faithfully and be committed to bearing the steadfast love you first showed us. May that be our legacy.

NOW AND LATER

*"What profit is it to a man if he gains the whole world,
and is himself destroyed or lost?"*
LUKE 9:25 NKJV

The world shakes its head at us in bewilderment when we exchange what is tangible for what is unseen, the riches of this world for the blessings of God, and instant gratification for eternal promises. If you feel social pressure to appear as though you have it all together, ask God to help you let those feelings go. You don't need to keep up with the neighbors; you have a higher calling than that.

As God's children, we're created for a different kingdom. Don't lose yourself in the rat-race of this world. You can't take anything with you, and it will cost you all your time and effort. Are there things in this world keeping you from giving your all to Christ?

Father, our short lives and little problems seem so insignificant when we consider the bigger story you're unfolding, yet to you, we matter immensely. You care about our problems because you care about us, and you want to use our little lives for your kingdom. Please use us, Lord.

COMPLETION

I am sure of this, that he who began a good work in you
will bring it to completion at the day of Jesus Christ.
PHILIPPIANS 1:6 ESV

Most of us have unfinished projects laying around the house. We started them with good intentions, but distractions came up, motivation died down, and we failed to finish them. Some of us have relationships we've given up on because, frankly, we lost interest or something more exciting came along.

Unlike us, God always completes what he starts. He never gives up on us, and he never loses interest in us. He has started a work in each of us, and if we continue to follow him, he will absolutely finish this work.

Thank you for never giving up on us, God. We will continue to trust you to do the work in us that you started. When we get distracted with less important things, or we lose interest in you or your Word, please forgive us and reignite the fire within us. We want to grow in our maturity and our relationship with you until the day Christ Jesus returns.

DIVINE LOVE

"Love your enemies, do good to those who hate you,
bless those who curse you, pray for those who mistreat you."
LUKE 6:27-28 NIV

Godly love is a divine characteristic outside the nature and understanding of stubborn humanity. Loving our enemies and doing good to those who are unkind to us can only come in true sincerity through the love and strength given by God.

Godly love is not learned or earned; it is freely given to those who ask God for it. The divine love of God which flows freely to us can then flow freely out of us when our hearts place Christ at the center of everything. We who have experienced this great love know it is not based on our merit, or the merit of the receiver, but on the giver.

Heavenly Father, by faith in Christ, we have a new nature. Please make us more and more like you so we can love our enemies as well as our friends. We pray today for those who have mistreated us recently.

LOVE CONQUERS ALL

In all these things we are more than conquerors
through him who loved us.
ROMANS 8:37 ESV

How loved a person feels can influence their entire disposition. Many behavioral issues stem from feeling unloved and unworthy. Children who grew up in loving homes are more likely to be confident, functioning adults than children who grew up in dysfunctional or abusive homes. When someone feels loved, it can light a fire inside them to do more, be more, and conquer more.

Love is a powerful thing! It can be stronger than guilt, shame, lust, and even self-preservation. God's love conquered death, and as his children, he pours his love into us. What are you going to do with that great gift today? How can you share his love?

Lord, your love for us is immense. Thank you for the work you accomplish in us by teaching us to love likewise.

TRUTH IN LOVE

Speaking the truth in love, we will grow to become in every respect the mature body of him who is the head, that is, Christ.

EPHESIANS 4:15 NIV

People love being right. They can't stand being wrong, and they can't stand being disagreed with by other people who similarly think they are right. The sad thing is that whoever has the right truth barely matters when opinions are hateful.

When we have those moments of triumph when we wipe the smirk off of someone's face as we prove them wrong or sinful, we are shriveling and burning our own souls. We are like children who have lost the ability to grow. It is only through "speaking the truth in love" that "we will grow to become in every respect the mature body" of Christ. We grow through humility, not pride. We grow through the choice to stand up and speak with humility and genuine concern for others rather than pride. If we desire Christ and want to be like him, our first step is to put away pride and contempt and put on the truth in love.

God, help us today in our interactions with each other. May we not seek to be right for the sake of triumph but for the sake of love. Teach us to emulate you in our interactions and become more like you through them.

TOP OF MIND

I lie awake thinking of you,
meditating on you through the night.
Because you are my helper,
I sing for joy in the shadow of your wings.
PSALM 63:6-7 NLT

As Christians, maintaining a close relationship with God is our first and primary calling. We are always on the Lord's heart, and he wants that same captivated love from us. Moreover, if we truly understood his majesty, we would be utterly, constantly enthralled.

Do you remember feeling mesmerized by your spouse when love was new and unexplored? Do you remember lying awake thinking about them? Perhaps familiarity calms our excitement, but it shouldn't dull our love. Tonight, try to lie awake and think of all the great things you love about your spouse even if they are lying next to you. Try to fill your mind with all the great things you love about God too. You will never run out of attributes that amaze you and make you grateful for the God we serve.

We are truly captivated by you, Lord. Our minds are consumed with thoughts of your greatness and grace. You have been our helper in our marriage, ministry, and self-improvement. Please continue to help us as we fall more and more in love with you over the years.

ACCEPTING EACH OTHER

Accept one another, then,
just as Christ accepted you,
in order to bring praise to God.
ROMANS 15:7 NIV

It is God's desire that we learn to live together in peace and harmony. His heart's desire is that we learn to accept each other's differences. This does not mean condoning sin, but it does mean recognizing that our way isn't always the best or only way. We each have different gifts, differing perspectives, and minds that work in unique ways.

God's Word is truth, and it offers us a standard for morality. As far as our individual callings and the application of our gifts, we all play different parts. Let's praise God for our differences, accept each other in our unique callings, and offer what support we can for the sake of God's glory and our harmony.

Teach us to value and trust each other, God. We know you made us unique and, especially in marriage, we recognize that we need these differences.

ABOVE ALL ELSE

"If you love your father or mother more than you love me, you are not worthy of being mine; or if you love your son or daughter more than me, you are not worthy of being mine."

MATTHEW 10:37 NLT

A strong marriage depends on a strong foundation, and there is none stronger than the one we find in Christ. In fact, when we are grounded in Christ and understand his character, our love for him will be so strong that any other love we possess will pale in comparison. We love the people in our lives, and we love God even more when we remember that it is he who established those relationships.

Only by loving God and experiencing his love can we love others including our spouses. If we want the full, abundant experience of a godly marriage, we should not only believe in Jesus for eternal life but also seek to follow him and be his loving disciples. He matters above all else.

Father, may our love for you grow and grow on this beautiful journey of knowing you better. Thank you for all the relationships you have given us too.

PICK UP YOUR SHIELD

As for God, His way is perfect;
The word of the LORD is proven;
He is a shield to all who trust in Him.
PSALM 18:30 NKJV

Are there struggles you are trying to face on your own? Pick up your shield, dear Christian. The Lord your God is mighty! He fights for you, and he has promised to protect you. His Word is proven, and his way is perfect. You can rest in him. He gives everything you need to walk in godliness if you take the time to listen to him and learn to use his tools. What's more, he has given you a spouse to confide in and lean on. Your spouse is a gift from God.

Marriage is a tangible way God shares his love with us, and he paints an image of what a holy union looks like. We were never meant to walk alone. Our loving God gives us himself, friends, family, a church body, and oftentimes a spouse. None of these gifts should be ignored or taken lightly. Praise God for his presence, his Word, and his way.

Thank you, Lord God, for being present and active in our lives. As we walk in your way and learn from your Word, we learn to put our faith in you. It becomes a shield able to withstand all the evil this world throws against us.

NEW LIFE

Throw off your old sinful nature and your former way of life, which is corrupted by lust and deception. Instead, let the Spirit renew your thoughts and attitudes. Put on your new nature, created to be like God—truly righteous and holy.

EPHESIANS 4:22-24 NLT

Accepting the invitation into God's family means taking off our former way of life and, by the power of the Holy Spirit, severing ourselves from our sinful behavior. It means entering into precious union and sweet communion with our Savior, Jesus Christ. Accepting God as our King does not simply mean we changed our minds but also our earthly citizenship and way of living.

When we are born again, the Spirit works in us to change our entire way of thinking and gives us a new, beautiful focus. How does walking in your inheritance as a child of God impact your life? Your job? Your marriage? Your finances? Your decisions and path forward?

Thank you for our new life and position in your family, Lord God. Today we commit to casting aside our old, self-centered way of living in favor of your better, eternal way.

UNDER PRESSURE

"Blessed are those who are persecuted for righteousness' sake,
For theirs is the kingdom of heaven."
MATTHEW 5:10 NKJV

What others may call injustice or offense, Christians recognize as opportunity. Anybody can profess faith, but faith under fire is where true testimony lies. It may be as simple as being the bigger person in an argument by apologizing or remaining calm, or it could be as extreme as being killed for our faith.

Whatever the case, Christians ought to act, speak, and walk differently than the world, and this is never more obvious than when the pressure is on. When a national crisis hits or a personal tragedy befalls us, others can be amazed and confused by our inner peace and ability to hold on to hope in any situation. This is because we know, in the end, everything will turn out right. We are blessed; we inherit the kingdom of heaven.

When the pressure is on, Lord God, remind us how important our testimony is. May we not lose sight of the bigger truth that you always protect and provide for your children. When we're subjected to terrible treatment here on earth, may others marvel at our confidence in you, not because we're great, but because we know how great you are.

WHOEVER LOVES GOD

This commandment we have from him:
whoever loves God must also love his brother.
1 JOHN 4:21 ESV

What is the evidence of our love of God? What measurement do we have? Christians sing and talk all the time about their love of God and how he enraptures and completes them. The commandment here is a conviction to show how much we love our Lord not by way of mouth service but by brotherly service.

If we love God, we will want to follow his commandments. His commandments are not burdensome; they set us free from our pride. It is not an option to love one person and not the other; God commands we love our brothers and sisters as we love him. As an earlier verse in 1 John says, anyone who says he loves God but does not love those around him is a liar.

Oh Lord, convict us to love everyone because of our compelling love for you. Give us the power to show no partiality and to extend grace and forgiveness out of our gratitude for what you have done for us. In doing so, people will know we love you.

INTENTIONALLY

Above all else, guard your heart,
for everything you do flows from it.
PROVERBS 4:23 NIV

Daily, earth's influences come at us from all directions and try to pull our attention away from God's eternal purposes. Did you know he has an eternal purpose for you? For your marriage? Even for today? There is a reason you exist right where you are.

We need to be careful what we allow into our lives and marriages. As Christians, we are people of purpose and direction despite the world wandering around us. We live in this world but not for this world. Let's strive to use our time on earth tending others with hearts full of love and pure intention and souls full of joy for the good news of salvation.

Dear Lord, thank you for another day in which we get to learn and love. Keep our hearts clean and full of the joy only you can give. Our intention is to live motivated by love for you and others and free from the vices of the world. Please guide and protect us through it all.

Without Complaint

Do all things without complaining and disputing.
PHILIPPIANS 2:14 NKJV

Grumbling reveals room for growth. Mature adults talk out their problems for the sake of finding solution and not to fill the air with negativity. The temptation to be heard and pitied may result in complaining which is not edifying to the hearer, the complainer, or God.

We who are married know that the hearer of our complaining is most often a spouse, and it can be a heavy load to carry. Instead of putting that weight on our spouses, let's bring our burdens to God and find real relief from their weight. Our spouses are there to help us, but God is there to solve the problems.

Loving Father, we confess that our sinful nature is prone to complaints and disputes. We recognize this is a display of pride and does not show trust in you. Please teach us to take every thought captive, moment by moment, and enable us to cast our cares on you. You know how to shoulder them far better than we do.

Rooted in Christ

As you received Christ Jesus the Lord, so walk in him, rooted and built up in him and established in the faith, just as you were taught, abounding in thanksgiving.

Colossians 2:6-7 esv

We are called to walk worthy of our Lord and to be fruitful in our Christian life. This is only achievable when we abide in him, trust our lives to his safekeeping, and walk in purity and truth. When we willingly choose to submit to the leading and guidance of the Holy Spirit in our lives, we can walk worthy of our Lord.

As believers, we have trusted Christ for salvation, but do we also trust him with our day-to-day happenings? We have given our lives to him, but do we give him our moments and decisions? Do we trust him with our money, our marriages, and our ministry? Our health and our families? That is what it means to walk in him.

Gratefully, God, we come to you today. We are rooted in you, so please build us up in your way instead of ours. Faith in you is more for us than the lessons we've been told; our faith is experienced every time we relinquish our wills to your better way.

WATCH AND CARRY

If anyone is caught in any transgression, you who are spiritual should restore him in a spirit of gentleness. Keep watch on yourself, lest you too be tempted. Bear one another's burdens, and so fulfill the law of Christ.
GALATIANS 6:1-3 ESV

Christian love, when carried out, helps carry others' burdens and can eliminate a multitude of potential sins. Christian love seeks to encourage others toward godly living and spiritual growth. We have been equipped to restore each other in a spirit of gentleness and love by the leading of the Holy Spirit.

Someone who is truly mature does not drag their spouse down with judgmental accusations. Instead, they offer encouragement and edification with the hope of helping restore them to their stronger standing.

Oh Lord, please give us your wisdom to know when and how we can help restore someone in the faith. Help us be kind, compassionate, hospitable, and gracious toward each other and anyone else who needs it. May we stay watchful and humble and not fall into temptation ourselves.

PROPER PRIORITIES

Guard the good deposit that was entrusted to you—
guard it with the help of the Holy Spirit who lives in us.
2 TIMOTHY 1:14 NIV

Having proper priorities is important; what you prioritize shapes you. Aligning your priorities with your spouse's priorities is just as important because your marriage will be influenced by where you spend your time. Activities can add up, and time with your spouse drops on the list of priorities, just like time with God does when our lives become too busy.

In Matthew 6:33, Jesus promises that if we're seeking the kingdom of God, the eternal things which matter to the heart of God, he will take care of all the rest. Likewise, let's prioritize time with our spouses. Lots of those other things will work themselves out if we're happily and healthily married.

Lord, we will always prioritize spending time with you. On the days we fool ourselves into thinking it's less of a priority, please step in and remind us. We will also prioritize spending time with each other because we recognize the gift you've given us through this marriage, and we want to honor and tend to it.

LIVING HONORABLY

Pray for us, for we are sure that we have a clear conscience,
desiring to act honorably in all things.
HEBREWS 13:18 ESV

Nothing is more upsetting than a guilty conscience. It can keep us from falling asleep or wake us in the middle of the night. That churning, sick feeling of a lack of peace whispers that the relationship is irreparable, that the small issue is actually enormous, or that we're terrible people.

Doing the right thing doesn't always produce the immediate outcome we desire, but it is preferable to living under the weight of guilt or regret. We are called to be faithful to God no matter the outcome, keep our conscience clear, and act honorably. The hope and sure future we have in God should transform our daily lives as we worry less about things important to the world and think more about what will last eternally.

Lord, thank you for your Word which helps us discern right from wrong. We desperately want to be honorable, keep our consciences clear, and always do the right thing. Please help us; we can't do it without you.

Understanding Love

I pray that you, being rooted and established in love, may have power, together with all the Lord's holy people, to grasp how wide and long and high and deep is the love of Christ, and to know this love that surpasses knowledge—that you may be filled to the measure of all the fullness of God.

Ephesians 3:17-19 niv

There is nothing mercurial about God's love. It is not based on whims, feelings, or passing fancies. His love is absolute regardless of the cost or of our behavior toward him. God's love never fails, never ends, and far surpasses any worldly love or knowledge we could find. Sin may incur his wrath, but like any good parent, it does not diminish his love.

We are all born with a need to be loved. We long to find someone who accepts us completely and who is worthy of our trust. Family, friendships, and romantic relationships are important, but they can't replace the love of our Creator. What we are truly looking for comes only from our heavenly Father.

Almighty God, you fill us with a love so secure we have the confidence to love others. Your love draws us closer together in love for each other and a shared love for you. Please keep us close to your heart.

FELLOWSHIP

Every day they continued to meet together in the temple courts. They broke bread in their homes and ate together with glad and sincere hearts, praising God and enjoying the favor of all the people. And the Lord added to their number daily those who were being saved.

ACTS 2:46-47 NIV

Before getting married, most people enjoy each other's company and spend lots of time together. Usually this continues into the early years of the marriage, but at some point, the responsibilities of life eat up the time. Other things crowd the relationship and take up the time that was originally spent together. Depending on how hectic our lives get, a husband and wife will find less and less time for each other because of jobs, children, projects, and other responsibilities.

It becomes increasingly difficult to spend time together as a married couple. We must, however, be deliberate in spending time together just as the disciples devoted time to meeting together. Carving out time to talk with each other, eat together, and fellowship both as a couple and as believers is key to keeping the furnace going.

Lord, thank you for fellowship we have in marriage. Spending time together is what you intend for us as husband and wife, and we need each other's presence to understand the blessing that is our relationship. Let us not get distracted or forsake spending this time together.

DEVOTION TO GOD

"No one can serve two masters, for either he will hate the one and love the other, or he will be devoted to the one and despise the other. You cannot serve God and money."

MATTHEW 6:24 ESV

Devotion to God needs to be paramount for our well-being. The world's systems often contradict God's ways, so devotion to both God and the world is not possible. There will come times when we need to choose between the easier, more instantly gratifying path of going along with the world or instead uphold our devotion to God and honor God through our decisions.

Money, for example, can be used for many great things. We need money to live on earth, but there is a difference between us using money and money using us. Have you submitted your bank account to the will of God? Not just ten percent but all of it? If we say we serve God and are devoted to him, we will hold nothing back in service to ourselves.

Search our hearts, dear God, and dig out anything not submitted to you. We don't want to hold anything back. All our money and possessions are at your disposal. After all, everything we have is thanks to you.

RENEWED STRENGTH

Those who wait on the LORD
Shall renew their strength;
They shall mount up with wings like eagles,
They shall run and not be weary,
They shall walk and not faint.

ISAIAH 40:31 NKJV

Hope in the Lord is like fuel for the believer. We rise and soar on the strength of the Holy Spirit, unable to accomplish anything which matters in our own strength yet flying above the troubles of this world on the wings of the Spirit of God. Christ strengthens us and raises us up. He renews us when we feel weary and when we patiently wait for him instead of trying to take matters into our own hands.

Are you tired today? Do you have problems you can't solve? Pray and wait patiently. Waiting does not mean giving up or doing nothing; it means having peace amidst hard work and knowing that God is going to bring it all together. May hope breathe new life into your marriage and family today.

Dear Lord, thank you for the strength you give us each morning to walk through the day and face any challenges brought by the world. Without your guidance and continued leadership, we would not be where we are now. We are eternally grateful.

Enduring Hope

Hope does not disappoint, because the love of God has been poured out in our hearts by the Holy Spirit who was given to us.

ROMANS 5:5 NKJV

Hope is the driving force behind our life choices and commitments. We hope for better days, for good to reign, and for eternal life with no stain of sin. A marriage between believers is based on this sort of hope, and a union centered on God will grow stronger each day. The Lord instills hope in our hearts and fills us with love and faith. When we encounter despair and dejection, as everyone will, the Holy Spirit reminds us of his love and hope which will last longer than pain.

Although we hope in our spouses, every human relationship will disappoint us at times. We need hope in the Lord as the backbone of our lives and marriages. The Lord's hope will never let us down. He always has been, and always will be, faithful to what he has promised.

Dear Lord, thank you for new beginnings, next mornings, and fresh starts. On this day, we are grateful for the gift of hope you've given us. We know you guide us and protect us at all times. We do not take it for granted, and we don't take your love for us for granted. We will always be thankful to you.

November

Love does not demand its own way.

It is not irritable, and it keeps

no record of being wronged.

1 Corinthians 13:5 NLT

SUBMISSION

*Submit to God. Resist the devil
and he will flee from you.*
JAMES 4:7 NKJV

We have a cunning enemy who wants nothing more than to destroy us because we reflect the Father. One sure way of infuriating him even further is when we act like our Father. In fact, he is left powerless when confronted with our almighty God, so when we are submitted to God and standing by his side, the devil has no choice but to run away.

God has given us a tangible way of submitting to him by gifting us marriage partners. If we love God, we will in turn love the son or daughter he entrusts to us. If we are honestly submitted to God, we will submit to each other as well. To draw closer to God and turn the devil on his heels, submit to your spouse's betterment, their needs, their godly desires, and their insight. Give yourself completely to God and to the person he knit you together with. Your enemy cannot stand against that.

Thank you, God, for standing up for us and giving us someone to stand with us. We want to show you how grateful we are and how submitted to you we are. One way we commit to showing you this is within our marriage.

RESOLUTE

"If you want to be my disciple, you must, by comparison, hate everyone else—your father and mother, wife and children, brothers and sisters— yes, even your own life. Otherwise, you cannot be my disciple."
LUKE 14:26 NLT

Marriage vows include the importance of forsaking all others in favor of the one person you have chosen to love. This means you have made up your mind to set your absolute favor upon this beloved soul, and you choose now to walk this road of life together. You both promise to stay faithful to the very end of one of your lives, and no other person has the right to break those vows.

Marriage calls us to be clear-headed about what we have decided to do. The same serious intentionality applies if we are not ready to commit to a beloved. We must be prepared for the gravity of the vows in order to have a holy marriage.

Lord, thank you for the calling you have placed on us concerning our lives in following you and concerning our marriage. Turn our gaze forward once we decide to follow your steps and commit to our marriage. As time goes by, may our gaze still be forward. Let us honor you and each other and be faithful to the end.

RIGHT LOVE

Do not love the world nor the things in the world.
If anyone loves the world, the love of the Father is not in him.

1 JOHN 2:15 NASB

There are objects undeserving of our love. Often, we think so much about the right way to love that we neglect to see some things are not worthy of our love. The world, as created by God in perfection, is a thing to be amazed by and wondered at. This is not the world that John is speaking about. He is speaking about the world of the devil, the corrupt side of the world defined by evil and temptation.

This world is not worthy of our love or adoration. It is easy to love because Satan makes it so, but it is not God's desire for us to love it. In fact, for us to love this world, we must give up "the love of the Father" because they are diametrically opposed. A similar situation exists within marriage. Just because it might feel right to grow a romantic interest in someone who is not a spouse does not make it a loving act. It might have a sort of love, yes, but it is not the love of the Father; it is a corrupted love that neglects the needs of a spouse in favor of someone else.

God, give us right love. Teach us to love what is worthy of love and to look past what is not. May we always love one another rightly.

OVERFLOWING LOVE

May the Lord make your love increase and overflow for each other
and for everyone else, just as ours does for you.
1 THESSALONIANS 3:12 NIV

Where do you turn to find meaning, relief from suffering, and satisfaction from the emptiness every person feels from time to time? What occupies your heart? Who consumes your thoughts, energy, and focus? If our whole lives are about ourselves, then we have a poor reason for existence. If we are so consumed with our spouses or the rest of our family that they are all we care about, that is a temporary calling.

When we find our purpose in God, however, we involve ourselves in something eternal and worth our while. From that great love and calling comes all the love we need for our family and ourselves. God guards us and our inheritance with him in eternity. He is the only assured place for us to set our hope, and his love extends to all other loves. Only in him can our hearts be fully satisfied.

Lord, thank you for life, our marriage, and all the other wonderful relationships you've blessed us with. As much as we love them, our greatest love is for you. Please fill us to overflowing with your love.

GOD ENTHRONED

In God, whose word I praise,
In God I have put my trust;
I shall not be afraid.
What can mere mortals do to me?
PSALM 56:4 NASB

There is nothing we need to be afraid of because God is on the throne. The most hideous acts and evil plots cannot stand against the Almighty or his anointed. Have you placed your trust in him? Are you daily reading his Word, hiding it in your heart, and praising him for its truths?

Since we are God's beloved bride, we do not need to be afraid, but that doesn't mean we won't be afraid. If we are not spending time with him in prayer and in the Scriptures, we are more apt to believe the enemy's lies and fear his empty threats. When the world around us is in chaos, it quickly reveals our faith and how much we trust our heavenly Father to preserve and protect us.

Cast fear away from us, dear Father. We know we have no need to be afraid, yet sometimes we are. Please help us gain better perspective and remind us how wonderful and powerful you are.

FLOODED WITH LIGHT

I pray that your hearts will be flooded with light so that you can understand the confident hope he has given to those he called.
EPHESIANS 1:18 NLT

Our eyes tend to adjust to darkness and light once we've sat in either one for a while. Darkness, like sin, seems less dark the longer you walk in it. Have you noticed that? The longer you walk in sin, the more you will learn to live with it. You will make excuses for it; your heart will adjust.

God has called us out of darkness and into his light. The longer we walk in light, the more acclimated our eyes become to it as well. His incredible love and majesty begin to seem more commonplace, and our hearts grow complacent. We are children of light, but we only see the greatness of God dimly at present. One day, we will see him as he is. Until then, let's often revisit his wonderous character, flood our hearts with light, and be awed by his glory and grace.

Don't let our hearts grow dim, dear Father. Remind us again and again of your glory and flood our hearts with your majestic light.

Our Merciful God

The steadfast love of the Lord never ceases;
his mercies never come to an end;
they are new every morning; great is your faithfulness.

LAMENTATIONS 3:22-23 ESV

If God does not answer you the way you expected or hoped for, don't become discouraged. Take a moment to remember all the ways he has come through for you in the past. His goodness doesn't change. Our situations might shift, but his love is steadfast, and his mercy is fresh every day.

We each have shortcomings and limitations, but God has neither. When we begin to grasp just how awesome and faithful our God is to us, we can relax in the knowledge he will answer in his way, his better way, when the time is right.

Heavenly Father, you are a gracious, loving, and long-suffering God. Help us not be influenced by the circumstances of life but instead keep our eyes on you. We know your plans and purposes are perfect.

STRENGTHS AND WEAKNESSES

Finally, all of you, be like-minded, be sympathetic,
love one another, be compassionate and humble.
1 PETER 3:8 NIV

In marriage, as with any relationship, both parties bring strengths and weaknesses to the relationship. God calls us to take our very different minds and work toward unity. It's important that our differences are used for the well-being of the marriage and the building of our relationship.

This is seen in today's verse. When spouses show each other sympathy, tender hearts, and humble minds, the marriage is strengthened within and shown to be honorable from without. This is incredibly important not just for the steadfastness of your marriage but also for your relationship with God. Anything that may cause friction and unnecessary tension in marriage should be avoided. Instead, the focus should be on channeling both strengths and weaknesses, so they are edifying to yourselves and God.

Lord, we learn in the Word that our strengths and weaknesses should be managed to edify our marriage as well as our relationship with you. Help us fulfill this task in a way that honors each other and brings glory to you.

REMEMBER ALWAYS

"Can a mother forget the baby at her breast and have no compassion on the child she has borne? Though she may forget, I will not forget you! See, I have engraved you on the palms of my hands; your walls are ever before me."

ISAIAH 49:15-16 NIV

God's remembrance never fades. For the human brain, memory works like a game of telephone. Every time we remember something, we are actually remembering the last time we remembered it which is why our memories get distorted with age. This is not the case with the memory of God. His memory is unchanging, and his ability to watch over us never fades. He is the only one we can fully rely on without any doubt.

When our spouses fail us or shirk their duties, we have God as an emblem of unshakeable dedication. This is the emblem we should aim to live up to. We should have the promise to cherish and respect our spouses metaphorically engraved on the palms of our hands. Our commitment to them is only true commitment if it is always in practice and never put aside.

Oh Lord, thank you for your perfect memory. We praise you because your incredible love for us never weakens. Your faithfulness is not temperamental or subject to change. It is always there and always dependable.

FEARLESS

Even though I walk through the valley of the shadow of death,
I fear no evil, for You are with me;
Your rod and Your staff, they comfort me.

PSALM 23:4 NASB

When we learn to trust God, it changes the way we live, and the difference is evident to those around us. Our lives are a testimony to what has power over us: fear or faith. The psalmist is not promising that those who follow God will never feel fear but rather that we have no reason to fear evil because God is with us. That knowledge is a comfort in the midst of the darkest days and even in the face of death.

Living fearlessly is a practice of faith. It is an ongoing decision to place our trust in God, follow his lead, accept his disciplinary rod of correction, discover his comfort, and kick the evil one out of our life. There is freedom from fear, and it is only found in faith in God.

Oh Father, you truly are the Good Shepherd. Please lead us, correct us, comfort us, and protect us. Together, we look to you for direction in life and defense against the enemy. No matter how bleak things get, we will continue to trust you.

PITFALLS OF PRIDE

The reward for humility and fear of the LORD
is riches and honor and life.
PROVERBS 22:4 ESV

Fear of the Lord and humility are necessary for every Christian's life. If you want a good life, a happy marriage, and internal peace and contentment, it starts with a healthy fear of the Lord and humility. Pride is a terrible temptation, and it whispers that we ought to look out for ourselves, putt our desires before others, and serve our interests above our spouses'. In the end, pride will cost us God's eternal riches. If we want to continue to be sanctified, fear of the Lord is imperative.

The good news is that God is willing to help us overcome our pride. The more we seek him and learn about his character, the more our awe of his greatness will grow. Fear of God motivates us to consider him and others above ourselves. Humility of the heart will produce an outpouring of good and not evil. It will be a blessing to us, our spouses, and anyone else in our lives.

Father God, remind us of your awesomeness whenever we are tempted to succumb to pride. In difficult moments when we want to be self-seeking and follow our own whims, remind us of who you are and what you have called us to do.

Carry Our Crosses

"Whoever does not bear his own cross and come after me cannot be my disciple."
Luke 14:27 esv

Christ dealt with the problem of our salvation in a moment, once and for all, while nailed to the cross. This issue of our sanctification, however, is another matter altogether. Discipleship means that, day by day, we follow in our Savior's footsteps and identify with him. That includes identifying with his suffering. As we walk with our Savior, our hearts begin to hurt for the things that hurt his heart. We love the things he loves and hate the things he hates. Like him, we give up our lives, hypothetically or actually, depending on what is required.

Christ desires faithful disciples who are humble of heart and ready to surrender everything for his glory no matter the cost. That is what it means to carry our crosses and truly be Christ's disciples.

Holy Jesus, we can't thank you or praise you enough for what you did for us and what you continue to do. It is our greatest honor, dear Savior, to follow in your footsteps and lay our lives down for you—not just once but daily.

STEADFAST LOVE

The LORD is merciful and gracious,
slow to anger and abounding in steadfast love.

PSALM 103:8 ESV

Scripture has a lot to say about love and how we should act toward others, and the reason is because God is loving toward us. His love is resolute, and he looks on us with mercy and patience. If we are his children, shouldn't we treat others with the same love, mercy, grace, and patience that we have been shown?

That is our calling in marriage and our other relationships. When we remember to extend the same grace we have received, it no longer matters whether we feel like the other person deserves our love in that specific moment; God always deserves our obedience. Even in our faltering and wandering, the Lord still loves us, cares for our needs, and shows us compassion. We should seek to do the same for others.

Oh Lord, thank you for your never-ending care and compassion. Thank you for forgiving our sins and being patient with us as we learn to walk in the freedom you've given us. Thank you for this marriage and all the other relationships you have blessed us with. Please teach us how to love and listen.

Pursue Peace

*Pursue peace with all people, and the holiness
without which no one will see the Lord.*
HEBREWS 12:14 NASB

You can be right and still be wrong. What you believe may be factual, but your delivery or approach may be selfish and arrogant. God does not ask us to have the right answers all the time; he instructs us to pursue peace and holiness. Why? That is what he wants displayed for the world.

Our lives, especially our marriages, are supposed to be a picture of God's love to this lost and hurting world. Even if people believe there is a god, they may not realize the goodness, peacefulness, and holiness of the true God. That is where we come in. How we treat our spouses matters because our union with them is where our character witness begins. Live at peace with your spouse. Fight for that! Truth is important, but details often aren't.

Lord, when we are tempted to fight over petty details and things that don't matter, please remind us that the real fight is not against each other but against the one who wants to destroy us and tear down your image. Help us fight for peace and holiness in our marriage.

FULFILLMENT IN GOD

Look to the LORD and his strength;
seek his face always.
1 CHRONICLES 16:11 NIV

People frequently enter into a relationship with the presupposition that they will be wholly fulfilled by the other person. Our society paints a picture of finding "the one" as being equal to everlasting happiness and contentment. The truth is, we were never meant to obtain satisfaction from anyone other than the Lord. Putting the burden on your spouse spiritually, emotionally, or physically will strain the relationship. The Lord wants to be your fulfillment.

The best practice to better your relationship with your spouse is to make time to be in God's presence, to seek his will, and to worship him. Setting your expectations correctly will give you the ability to see your spouse for who they are meant to be: your helper in this life. The goal of marriage is to exemplify Jesus and his bride, and the only way we can learn to do that is by dwelling in the Word of the bridegroom himself.

Father, you are the culmination of the peace and satisfaction we seek. We find our fulfillment in you alone. Help us free each other from the pressure we impose on one another. We commit ourselves to you first and foremost.

GREATER GLORY

I consider that the sufferings of this present time are not worth comparing with the glory that is to be revealed to us.
ROMANS 8:18 ESV

Hope is a driving spirit when things are not going well. It sustains us when times are gloomy and dark. Suffering in a believer's life has the blessing of a background of hope. Throughout a marriage's challenges and when we are overwhelmed, hope keeps us going. It's a force that pushes us through hard times and the various obstacles in the life of a marriage.

Today's verse tells us that the sufferings of this present time pale in comparison to the glory which will be revealed to us later. We have hope for a more glorious tomorrow where all the suffering and pain of our present life will be distant memories.

Lord, thank you for the assurance you give in our present suffering. Your Word tells us worldly pain can't compare to the glory to come. Thank you for the hope that resides in us and keeps us going when things are hard. This knowledge lets us focus on the prize of our eternal lives.

ONE BODY ONE SPIRIT

There is one body and one Spirit—just as you were called to the one hope that belongs to your call—one Lord, one faith, one baptism, one God and Father of all, who is over all and through all and in all.

EPHESIANS 4:4-6 ESV

When God instituted the first marriage, he explained that the husband and wife would become like one flesh (Gen 2:24). The same sentiment is seen in our inclusion within the population of true believers worldwide. In this body of Christ, we share the same hope, the same upward calling, and the same love for our Father God.

Therefore, we uphold relationships as God does by maintaining peace and sacrificial love. This includes the union between us as married couples and between us and our brothers and sisters in the faith.

Heavenly Father, thank you for your Word which reveals your will to us. As we learn, we commit to revering our marriage union and our position in the broader body of believers.

ETERNAL INHERITANCE

Day by day the LORD takes care of the innocent,
and they will receive an inheritance that lasts forever.
They will not be disgraced in hard times;
even in famine they will have more than enough.

PSALM 37:18-19 NLT

Food only fills us for a moment, but the Lord's sustenance sustains us forever. God promises to uphold the innocent, and if we have accepted Christ's forgiveness, we are deemed innocent. There are evil people in this world who seem to hold all the cards, but their reign is restricted to their short lives on earth and all the enjoyment they can stuff into their limited years.

The inheritance of Christ is for all eternity, and he gladly includes his faithful followers in it. Worldly power looks alluring, but what is currently unseen, stored in heaven for the redeemed, is what will ultimately last. In the meantime, the Lord's goodness preserves us day by day.

Oh God, may we not become star-struck by the apparent power of the world's esteemed. You alone hold all the cards. Thank you for taking care of us each and every day and including us in your eternal inheritance.

MADE RIGHT

He will bring out your righteousness as the light,
And your judgment as the noonday.
PSALM 37:6 NASB

All will be made right. One day, when Jesus comes back, those who have put their trust in him will be perfected, and the good work he began in each of us will be completed.

This verse has the power to give us great peace. The many injustices in our world seem devastatingly evil, but we know God is going to make all things new. The evil in the world will be banished forever. God, who put the sun in its place and causes it to rise every morning and set every night, will also bring about the ultimate form of justice. Our struggle with sin will be over, pain will cease, and the vulnerable will be safe.

God, thank you for this reminder that the struggle will one day be over. Help us stand strong while we wait for that day. Teach us how to encourage and strengthen each other in the truth of your coming return.

LOVE MADE PERFECT

Love has been perfected among us in this: that we may have boldness in the day of judgment; because as He is, so are we in this world.
1 JOHN 4:17 NKJV

When life is at its easiest, it is natural to think of ourselves as being good. We are the heroes of our stories, virtuous and godly. However, trials and tribulations reveal our true character. John says that now, our time on earth, is the time when our love is made perfect. The love we show at our most ill-tempered moments is the real love.

It's bold to say the perfection of our love occurs on earth and not in heaven. God is perfect in his love above, but we are to reflect his image on earth. We must reflect this image of love now while life is difficult and our mortal bodies weigh us down. We can't share this image just to those at work or in society; we must show it to those closest to us too. If we commit ourselves to loving our spouses when things are difficult, we will reap the benefits of perfect love when things are beautiful.

God, give us faith for we have none without your help. Give us the faith to perfect our love here on earth when things are difficult so we may bold on the day of judgment.

BEYOND SELF

Love one another with brotherly affection.
Outdo one another in showing honor.
ROMANS 12:10 ESV

Some things should happen without discussion in the context of marriage. For instance, we should be devoted to each other in love. We should also put our spouses above ourselves. It's worth emphasizing these points because behaving this way does not come naturally to most of us. The human condition makes it challenging to put someone's else interests above your own, but that is what marriage is all about. It calls on us to consider our spouses as deserving of our devotion and make the effort to honor them above ourselves.

It is the goal of a righteous, biblical marriage that we aspire to the example Christ has with the church. This is our reference point of what love and honor should look like and require. Today and every day in our marriage, let us seek to edify and lift each other up in love, honor, and devotion.

Lord, in your Word, you tell us to be devoted to and honorable toward each other above ourselves. This is the example you demonstrated to us by calling the church your bride. Give us your Spirit who loves above all and enables us to be better than our human inclinations would allow.

DO GOOD

Do not forget to do good and to share,
for with such sacrifices God is well pleased.
HEBREWS 13:16 NKJV

God created us for community, not for isolation, and with community come all the ins and outs of relationships. Beginning with our immediate family and working outwards, God has called us to do good and share. Everything we have was entrusted to us by him, and to him we are responsible for its use.

Doing good may look different at different times and with different people. For your spouse, the most impactful good may be in the small things like doing the dishes, offering heartfelt compliments, giving them a back rub, or praying for them often. Do good for them that speaks love to them in the way they want to receive it. For other people, it may mean digging deep into our pockets or our schedules and sharing our precious money or time. It may mean giving a listening ear or volunteering. When we give ourselves to strengthen others, that is an offering pleasing to God.

Lord, thank you for calling us together in marriage. Please teach us more about each other and show us ways we can do good and share with one another.

Inner Beauty

Don't be concerned about the outward beauty of fancy hairstyles, expensive jewelry, or beautiful clothes. You should clothe yourselves instead with the beauty that comes from within, the unfading beauty of a gentle and quiet spirit, which is so precious to God.

1 Peter 3:3-4 NLT

We all strive to appear more attractive. Some people work hard to maintain themselves by working out, grooming well, and so forth. Others perhaps don't get much further than brushing their hair and their teeth. Wherever we fall on the physical care spectrum, we all understand that it takes work and maintenance.

Inner beauty is no different; it also requires hard work and maintenance. How dedicated are we to keeping up our inner beauty and fostering a gentle and quiet spirit? Is your spirit quiet, or is it filled with all the world's noise? Inner beauty doesn't fade with time as physical beauty will. Many people undergo painful or expensive enhancements and procedures to aid in their physical appearance, but these will fade too. Let's make sure our unfading, precious inner beauty is a higher priority to us, and let's make a point to recognize the inner beauty and precious qualities of our spouses.

Oh Lord, give us eyes to see what's important and to appreciate the true beauty of ourselves and others.

PASSIONATE UNITY

May the God of patience and comfort grant you to be like-minded toward one another, according to Christ Jesus, that you may with one mind and one mouth glorify the God and Father of our Lord Jesus Christ.
ROMANS 15:5-6 NKJV

Unity comes from God's Spirit as we follow Jesus. Unity has a purpose deeper than simply getting along with other believers. It is a representation that we are from the same family: God's family. We want to be united so our cumulative praise brings glory to God.

Unity is more than an ideal; it's our calling. Unity is a process through which our marriage glorifies Jesus and declares to the surrounding world what it looks like to follow Jesus. God gives us the patience and courage to have fellowship with others, and together we become like-minded in our love for him and in adherence to his Word. Let's make unity our passion.

Almighty God, you offer strength to all who ask you for it, so we are asking for it today. Please give us patience and comfort in our relationships so we can worship and serve you together.

BEAR WITH EACH OTHER

We who are strong ought to bear with the failings of the weak
and not to please ourselves. Each of us should please our neighbors
for their good, to build them up.

ROMANS 15:1-2 NIV

Each of us has shortcomings, and these become apparent in marriage. Our response should not be to antagonize each other but to help each other out. Sometimes, that means allowing your spouse to do things their way instead of insisting it be done the way you would do it. Love, after all, does not insist on its own ways. Even God allows us to figure many things out our way even though he knows the best way.

The whole idea is to seek ways to build each other up. If you are strong for your spouse where they are weak, and they are strong for you where you are weak, you will have an unstoppably strong marriage, The two of you can then be a strength to others and help them where they are weak.

One day, wonderful Savior, you will return, and we will finally be perfected. Until then, thank you for having grace on our weaknesses. Thank you for giving us to each other so we can be stronger together. Teach us to have grace and love.

KEEP IT FRESH

Dear brothers and sisters, we urge you in the name of the Lord Jesus to live in a way that pleases God, as we have taught you. You live this way already, and we encourage you to do so even more.

1 THESSALONIANS 4:1 NLT

Isn't it refreshing to see Christians who are eager to learn and grow spiritually? It's most evident in new Christians. Why, as we grow older in the Lord, does it get easier to drift into a humdrum spiritual life? Shouldn't we be more eager and on fire after spending so much time with God? Why do we lose that zest to know him? Life becomes methodical, but the freshness of our first love for Christ shouldn't fade. To avoid this, we need to continually stoke the fire.

The same thing can happen in marriage. We can't maintain the euphoria first felt when love was new, but a routine relationship in which romance has faded is not acceptable either. To keep romance alive takes work and effort like it does in our spiritual lives. Let's deliberately stoke the fires of our relationships with God first and then our spouses.

Father God, you offer us a new opportunity each day to live intentionally. Every morning, we want to seek you anew. Remind us what a gift our marriage is so we treat it the way you intended.

ENTRUSTED

I am not ashamed, for I know whom I have believed,
and I am convinced that He is able to protect what
I have entrusted to Him until that day.

2 TIMOTHY 1:12 NASB

We often think about what God has entrusted to us, but what have you entrusted to him? Consider the outcome of investing in the kingdom of God. Can you imagine what that return would be?

You can't out-give God; he is infinitely generous. Just look at what he can do with a mustard seed. What could he do with a life of obedience? Or a marriage on fire for him? Or a family who puts him first? Think of how our lives would look if we fully entrusted ourselves to him. He is more than able to take care of everything. Let us unashamedly draw closer to our faithful God in confidence. Everything we place in God's hands will be the most worthwhile investment we ever make.

Take our lives, Lord God, and use them for your purposes. We give you our marriage because we want it to demonstrate our love for you. We entrust our entire family to you; please make use of us in your kingdom. All we have has been given to us by you, and we offer it back for your glory.

LOVE'S STRENGTH

Love is patient, love is kind. It does not envy, it does not boast, it is not proud. It does not dishonor others, it is not self-seeking, it is not easily angered, it keeps no record of wrongs.

1 CORINTHIANS 13:4-5 NIV

Often, we think of love in terms of passion, desire, or the will to do something. Love is a two-edged sword, and the passion of love is balanced by its quiet strength. When people would be impatient, rise to anger, or burn with envy, love is the power within them that holds them back. God chooses to manifest his love in people as self-control and better judgment. When people are loving, they can be angry or rude but choose not to.

The "nots" listed in this verse to the Corinthians are actions or emotions that make people feel more powerful. They are things people do to get back at people or to show they have been hurt. Those who love don't do these things. They have the wisdom to know they don't need to show off signs of strength; their strength is quiet.

Dear God, give us the love to not give in to negative reactions or lesser emotions. Give us the love to put others before ourselves and humbly show a quiet strength rather than rudeness and arrogance.

No Separation

"The glory that you have given me I have given to them, that they may be one even as we are one, I in them and you in me, that they may become perfectly one, so that the world may know that you sent me and loved them even as you loved me."

JOHN 17:22-23 ESV

The marriage union is God-ordained and should not be taken lightly. When two people join together, they are doing more than simply following their own desires for companionship. They are taking part in portraying the kind of love and union God intends for him and his people to share.

Marriage was designed to point us toward God's love and help us understand him better. The implications of a wedding are widespread, and the union is felt within the whole family and often the community. Marriages matter to God.

You are the author of marriage, God, and marriage matters immensely to you. We pray that our union brings you glory and honor. May we reflect your love.

BONDING TWO

The LORD God caused a deep sleep to fall upon the man, and while he slept took one of his ribs and closed up its place with flesh.
GENESIS 2:21 ESV

Man and woman are intrinsically meant to be with one another. The bond of marriage is not the bringing together of two separate people but rather the reconjoining of one thing. It must have been in the mind of God to include a few verses describing the world with a lonely Adam, but this was never meant to last. From the depth of the ages, he intended to institute marriage through the precedent of Adam and Eve.

Love is the force that spiritually reunites man and woman in every marriage. It is the source and sustenance of unity that flows from the heart of God and gives him glory through its display in holy marriage. The love one has for their beloved is the preservation of a holy and primal bond.

Holy Lord, how unsearchable are your thoughts and how intricate your designs! Every aspect of who we are is an echo of what you started in Eden long ago, and it continues to give you praise as it did then. Thank you, God, for the unity of man and woman.

DECEMBER

Above all, constantly echo God's

intense love for one another,

for love will be a canopy

over a multitude of sins.

1 PETER 4:8 TPT

BETTER THAN LIFE

Because Your lovingkindness is better than life,
My lips shall praise You.
PSALM 63:3 NKJV

Most of us do not describe things as being better than life. To say something is better than life means we would be willing to forfeit our own life in exchange for this valuable thing. This one thing has to be so valuable that we view life without it as worthless. The "lovingkindness" of God is that valuable. The psalmist would rather forfeit his life knowing God's lovingkindness was upon him than live a life without it. He would rather die in the Lord's arms than breathe the breath of the living. This lovingkindness of God, his tolerance and compassion for us, is so great that the psalmist has to praise. He is completely enraptured by God's undeserved grace.

When we focus our life on our spouses or our marriages, they are bound to fall apart. We are not big enough to navigate the emotional difficulties of marriage alone. If we want strong, secure marriages, we should live focused on the glorious truths of God and his great lovingkindness for us.

Lord, you are the perfection of every good thing in us. You are the glorious one, and for that we praise you.

DEVOTION

"The mountains may be removed and the hills may shake,
But My favor will not be removed from you,
Nor will My covenant of peace be shaken,"
Says the LORD who has compassion on you.

ISAIAH 54:10 NASB

Devotion is understood as fidelity, loyalty, love, and care for someone. Devotion is the story of God toward us. Even if everything else seems uncertain, God's devotion is assured. He made a covenant with us which he will never break. Whole mountains will break before God's promises do!

God does not take his covenant lightly and neither should we. When we accepted Jesus as our Lord and Savior, we entered into a covenant of love with God. When you looked your spouse in the eye and said, "I do," you entered into a covenant with them. Even when everything around you is falling apart, the future is uncertain, and dreams are shattered, stay devoted to your spouse. Do not shake in your covenants; the Lord is unwavering in his.

As we care for each other, fight for purity, and hold fast to our devotion for one another, we are constantly reminded of how you fight for us. Heavenly Father, your commitment to us gives us the confidence and strength to uphold our covenants as well.

FIRST THINGS FIRST

*"Seek first the kingdom of God and His righteousness,
and all these things shall be added to you."*

MATTHEW 6:33 NKJV

Everything in life has an order to it. It's important, through prayer and supplication to God, to get our priorities right. Things tend to fall into place if we have taken the time to prioritize a carefully considered order.

As believers, it's clear what the priority should be whether we are married, are about to get married, or maybe just thinking about it. Matthew 6:33 tells us that we must first seek the kingdom of God. It doesn't get clearer than this. In our lives, in our marriages, in everything, we need to seek God first. The beauty is that if we put God first in all things, the rest will be added. Trust God to give you a great, flourishing marriage when you seek him first.

Lord, we thank you for your Word which gives us good direction. Help us seek you before anything else. May we have our priorities in the right order and not fall into complacency or a lack of focus. Seeking you first will allow everything else to fall into place.

Pursuing and Finding

Whoever pursues righteousness and kindness
will find life, righteousness, and honor.
PROVERBS 21:21 ESV

The American ideal is to pursue what we want and get it. That is the hamster wheel most of our society runs in. It is a blessing to be able to work, get a fair wage, and experience the fruits of our labors, but sometimes pursuing one thing will get us something else. The writer in Proverbs tells us that if we want honor or life, we should pursue righteousness and kindness.

A person who pursues righteousness and kindness will indeed gain righteousness, but their level of character will also give them honor in the eyes of those around them. Righteousness and kindness also fill a person with life, healing the wounds of previous years and strengthening muscles that have atrophied. The journey in a relationship is similar to this. If we pursue our spouses as our highest goal, we will destroy the relationship. If instead we pursue God, along with his righteousness and kindness, we will find the healthy relationship we desire.

God, implant in us the wisdom to know what and what not to pursue. Make righteousness and kindness our highest priority above the unworthy things of this world.

OBEDIENCE

*"We must obey God rather than
any human authority."*
ACTS 5:29 NLT

Although we are to respect authority, maintain peace when possible, and obey human laws when we can, our final King is God, and we give our allegiance to his kingdom. Peter and the other disciples were faced with a decision to follow God or human leaders, and they knew held their loyalty.

Only one kingdom will stand forever. The Bible is clear we should obey earthly authorities whenever we can, but if their mandates contradict the laws of God, our decision (although potentially costly) should be easy. God's laws guide us on the straight and narrow and keep us from becoming lost or confused. His ways are always the best ways, and we can trust him.

If we ever come upon a moral crossroads, great King, and the laws of the land don't support your holy laws, please give us boldness and humility to stand for what is right. Help us obey you even when it's hard.

GOD HEARS

"You will call on me and come and pray to me, and I will listen to you."

JEREMIAH 29:12 NIV

Humans are petty creatures. We are constantly looking for ways to one-up each other. One of the most dangerous results of our desire for respect can come in the form of resentment and lack of forgiveness. When someone hurts us, we want them to feel the hurt they caused us. When they come back to us, even on their knees, there is the temptation to turn them away like they turned us away when we did not deserve it.

This pettiness is not fitting for Christians. Even God Almighty, who has never once been wrong, is willing to put his qualms aside for a humanity drenched in sin. He is willing to listen to us when we call on him. All he requires of us is a willingness to ask for forgiveness and enter into relationship with us. This is the example we should follow in our partnerships with other people and especially our spouses. God's connection to us is deep and emotional, just like a marriage bond, so he knows how much it hurts us when our partners say or do something against us.

God, please work in us to make us communicative, forgiving, and free of pride.

REMAINING HOLY

You must live as God's obedient children. Don't slip back into your old ways of living to satisfy your own desires. You didn't know any better then. But now you must be holy in everything you do, just as God who chose you is holy.

1 PETER 1:14-15 NLT

Everyone in Christ has a before and an after. There was a time, even if we were very little, before we trusted in Christ and did not know the truth. We did not understand. We lived in ignorance of what was real and what mattered. We followed our desires instead of God's desire for us. Without Christ in our lives, there was a void we were desperate to fill with anything else, but nothing fit. Nothing could satisfy. Our own human desires were to bring ourselves gratification and relief at any cost, so our lives began and ended with us.

Now that we are in Christ, we have been profoundly changed! We have become heirs of God who strive to obey him because of our heartfelt love and thankfulness. We live for a purpose greater than ourselves.

Lord, we are your children engulfed in love and thankfulness for all you have done. We want to obey you and live purely, so please help us because we know this is your desire too. Thank you for aligning our desires with yours.

HOPE

Whatever was written in earlier times was written for our instruction,
so that through perseverance and the encouragement
of the Scriptures we might have hope.

ROMANS 15:4 NASB

God is timeless, and God's Word is as relevant today as it was when it was written. The wisdom of the world changes with the emotional temperature of the culture. One moral may be trendy for a moment, but there will be a new theme next year.

Hope in humanity is futile because humans without God are bound to fail. Biblical hope is certain, however, because the promises of God are sure. God doesn't get caught up in the fashionable merits of the day; his Word has withstood the tests of time, and it will withstand the wiles of our generation as well. We can place our hope confidently in it.

Lord God, we are grateful for your Word. Without it, we would be lost people groping around in the dark with no hope, no direction, and no meaning. Your Word is life and light to all humankind. Thank you for the eternal hope you have given us.

BELONGING

*"My beloved is mine,
and I am his."*
SONG OF SOLOMON 2:16 NASB

At the heart of marriage is the concept of belonging to each other, not as owners of each other, but in a beautiful, healthy, freeing attachment. A husband and wife belong to each other just as Christ and the church belong to each other. There is a connection, a deep trust, and a love that binds them together.

It is a profound and wonderful gift that two people give each other in their marriage by loving each other in the way spoken about in the Song of Solomon. Spouses can belong to each other for a lifetime in such love and freedom when their marriage demonstrates Christ's love for the church as it was intended to do.

Lord, thank you for the gift of marriage. Thank you for bringing two people together from different backgrounds and families to love each other. May we grow closer in you, seek your guidance, and honor each other.

CONTENDING

Dear friends, I had been eagerly planning to write to you about the salvation we all share. But now I find that I must write about something else, urging you to defend the faith that God has entrusted once for all time to his holy people.

JUDE 1:3 NLT

Have you ever tried to accomplish something like a task, a chore, or a project and come up against resistance? The very nature of life is that anything worthwhile requires effort. You will come across resistance both within yourself as well as from conflicts around you. Marriage is no exception. Like anything else worth having, it demands effort, and we will meet resistance in the quest for a godly marriage.

The verse today addresses the need to contend for our faith. To contend means to strive or dispense effort for something. In this case it's referring to faith, but it can also be applied to marriage. We have to work on it because it's valuable and worthwhile. The very next verse, Jude 1:4, discusses the threat posed by ungodly people around us. They have plans to thwart our beautiful unions with efforts to introduce sensuality and deny our Lord, Jesus Christ. Our efforts to contend for our faith and our marriages are necessary in any day and age.

Lord, we know marriage is your creation and your plan for those called into it. Help us uphold, contend for, and value the union you have given us.

HARMONY

Mercy and truth have met together;
Righteousness and peace have kissed.

PSALM 85:10 NKJV

A beautiful bond is shared in marriage. When two people intertwine their lives together in love and with a common purpose, it is unlike anything else on earth. Several Bible passages touch on this including Psalm 85:10.

What a perfect picture of how God engulfs us in his mercy, truth, righteousness, and peace, and what the hallmarks of a Christian marriage should be as well. This is the perfect recipe for a strong, harmonious marriage, and we learned it all from God. As the Creator of marriage, God offers us all the ingredients to make our union flourish.

We praise you, Lord, for your perfect display of mercy, truth, righteousness, and peace. May we be faithful to show these same virtues to each other.

EXPRESSION OF LOVE

No one has ever seen God. But if we love each other,
God lives in us, and his love is brought to full expression in us.

1 JOHN 4:12 NLT

God isn't simply loving; God is love, and love is God. It originated with him, and he is the perfection of it. Although we've never seen God's face, we get to experience his character when we love others and are loved by them. The primary way Christians are recognized is by God's love. This is not merely what we feel but what we do for others. Love is proactive and not reactive.

Godly love is the most powerful evidence of being a child of God; it is his expression of himself through us to the world. How do you exemplify God's love? How do you love your spouse? Your family? Your neighbors? Your coworkers? Remember, love is actions more than it is feelings.

Dear heavenly Father, we thank you for all your good gifts like peace, hope, and faith, but most of all we thank you for your love. Help us share this love with actions and not just words. Thank you for choosing to express yourself through us. We are honored.

A Good Thing

He who finds a wife finds a good thing
and obtains favor from the LORD.
PROVERBS 18:22 ESV

The Lord calls each of us to different things, but there is no denying the blessing in having a spouse who loves and cares for you. We receive special favor from the Lord when we lay aside ourselves to love someone else, and it's required for a good marriage.

Do you recognize the added blessing your spouse brings to your life? Can you see the way God is at work between the two of you? Marriage is a remarkable way to learn how to put the needs of someone else above your own. Sometimes this is difficult to do, but that is why the Lord places added favor on us so we will have the grace and wisdom to do so.

Thank you for your favor, dear Lord. Thank you for all the amazing days the two of us have had. Thank you for giving us grace on hard days and forgiveness when we mess up. We truly need your favor, God. Marriage is not easy, but it's worth it.

SATISFY YOUR SOUL

Let them praise the LORD for his great love
and for the wonderful things he has done for them.
For he satisfies the thirsty and fills the hungry with good things.
PSALM 107:8-9 NLT

Have you ever eaten a good meal that didn't quite satisfy you? Marriage is a good meal, but only God can fill us to the brim with everything our souls yearn for, extinguish our loneliness, and refresh us daily. Your spouse is a wonderful gift from God, but he or she is not meant to take away your loneliness or satisfy your hunger. Your soul was made for God, and it is only he who can make it so you will never thirst or hunger again.

It is not fair to put this onus on another human. When God is the focus of your life and the one who answers your longing for purpose and love, then marriage can be treated as what it was meant to be: a gift from God to complement his work in you.

We praise you, almighty God, for the work you have done and are continuing to do in our hearts and in our marriage. Instead of placing an impossible burden on each other, we will look to you to satisfy our souls, and we will enjoy your wonderful gift of marriage.

LACK NOTHING

My brethren, count it all joy when you fall into various trials,
knowing that the testing of your faith produces patience.
But let patience have its perfect work, that you may be perfect
and complete, lacking nothing.

JAMES 1:2-4 NKJV

Doesn't it sound delightful to lack nothing? The world tells us we need to hustle to achieve all the things we think we need, but the Bible tells us that it's through patience that we will be made complete and lack nothing. Those are two very different approaches. The Bible is not saying we shouldn't work hard, but it is saying we ought not become impatient or frantic and lose sight of the one who actually fills our needs.

The world also wants us to believe that if something is hard, it's bad, and the easy life is what we should desire. However, we grow more through difficult times, and this verse tells us we should be joyful when trials and tests come our way because that's part of the journey toward completeness. Marriage can be difficult too. Rather than look for the easy way around, embrace the challenge, find joy in the work, and you will have as close to a perfect and complete marriage as one could hope to find.

Oh God, when our marriage gets rocky, we pray you will bring this verse to mind. We want to find joy even in the midst of difficult days. No marriage is perfect, but you are perfecting us. Thank you for the work you are doing in us and in our marriage.

DIRECTION

Lord, I know that people's lives are not their own;
it is not for them to direct their steps.
JEREMIAH 10:23 NIV

We all know what it's like for plans to change. It's doubtful any of us are exactly where we thought we would be ten years ago. The world teaches a mindset that is self-focused. It wants you to believe that your end motive should be your own happiness. As Christians, we know that's an empty, disappointing motive. We live for a purpose so much bigger than any one of us, and it fills us with a deeper joy when we are walking out in it.

When we got married, our plans certainly changed. Now, we can't live for only ourselves. Marriage is a wonderful way to learn how to live with others in mind, how to be flexible, and how to trust the Lord for leading and direction.

Lord, you have faithfully led us this year, and we trust you with this next year also. Help us learn not to hold on to our plans so tightly that we miss what you are doing. We trust you.

PATIENCE

God had mercy on me so that Christ Jesus could use me as a prime
example of his great patience with even the worst sinners. Then others
will realize that they, too, can believe in him and receive eternal life.

1 TIMOTHY 1:16 NLT

Have you ever had someone test your patience and push you to
the edge of doing something ugly? Isn't it incredible how God
keeps his cool when we are constantly testing his patience?

The apostle Paul understood this. He knew what a wretched,
murderous, arrogant sinner he was before Christ redeemed him. He
was quite sure that God chose him, the worst of all sinners, to be an
example to the onlooking world that anybody can be forgiven and
change. Patience, also known as forbearance or longsuffering, is a
fruit of the Spirit (Gal 5:22). It is a necessary quality to cultivate. In
this world, we're going to need a lot of it!

Lord, you have shown us amazing, unmerited mercy and
patience. As you have done for us, we want to do for
others. Beginning with each other, our closest ally and
friend in marriage, we will practice mercy and patience
by showing the same compassion you showed us.

ATTACHMENT

"'For this reason a man shall leave his father and mother
and be joined to his wife, and the two shall become one flesh'?
So then, they are no longer two but one flesh."
MATTHEW 19:5-6 NKJV

We are all attached to something or someone. Attachment is
the feeling that binds one to a person, a thing, a cause, or an
ideal. Such devotion in a relationship demonstrates an enduring
emotional bond between two people.

Scripture says that a man will leave his father and mother and
will cleave to his wife. The two of them then become one flesh. In
a Christian marriage, the husband's primary attachment should
be to his wife. That means that he will make a conscious effort to
make sure his wife is the primary emotional attachment in his life.
Sometimes family ties can hurt marriage if spouses are not careful.
Other attachments should fall lower in importance to the special
bond between husband and wife.

Lord, your Word says that a husband will leave
his father's house and then cleave to his wife, but
sometimes family ties can interfere with a marriage.
Please give us the clarity of mind to keep each other
and our marriage above other human relationships.

SOURCE OF LOVE

The one who does not love does not know God,
because God is love.

1 JOHN 4:8 NASB

How glorious it is to know that God is love and that the love we are called to manifest in our lives has its source in the divine love of God! It's amazing to realize that the outpouring of his unique love flows through us to others because we are his children.

Love is the basis of a Christian life and marriage. Human affection is nice for a time, but it can't satisfy our souls the way God's permeating, everlasting love can. Even the romantic love shared between a husband and wife, the devoted love a parent feels for their children, or the experienced love shared between long-time friends can't be confused with the divine love which has its singular source in God and is poured out on his children. Every other love stems from God's love.

May we increase in love in every area of our life and marriage, dear God, until we become transparent conduits through whom your divine love flows. Please use us to show your love to each other and others for your praise and glory.

GOD'S KINDNESS

Don't you see how wonderfully kind, tolerant,
and patient God is with you? Does this mean nothing to you?
Can't you see that his kindness is intended to turn you from your sin?
ROMANS 2:4 NLT

The reason we refuse to indulge in sin and take the narrower path of righteous living is not to earn our salvation. We are saved by God's rich kindness which draws us to repentance. It is his tolerance, not our good deeds, which saved us from our fate. A repentant heart is all he requires, and he is more than happy to patiently lead us the rest of the way.

This is not something we should take lightly, and we should not try to improve upon it by attempting to earn our chair at his table. God's system is not based on tallies, scores, or good deeds versus bad deeds. No, God's kingdom and its laws are based on love. In love, he came and rescued us because he knew anything less than perfect was not good enough, and he knew perfection was unattainable for us. His kindness, tolerance, and patience are the richest blessings in the world.

God, thank you for your kindness which drew us to you and for your tolerance and patience because you never give up on us. We know we're not perfect, but by your grace, we're being refined.

Stand Firm

*My beloved brothers and sisters, be firm, immovable,
always excelling in the work of the Lord, knowing that your
labor is not in vain in the Lord.*

1 Corinthians 15:58 NASB

Those who have given their allegiance to Christ have the glorious assurance that every promise of God will be fulfilled. Our trust in God's Word is steadfast, and our hope in Christ's return is guaranteed. No matter what trials and tribulations we face, we can stand firm in our immovable faith.

This sort of confidence propels us in the work of the Lord and our commitment to biblical values because we know our striving is not in vain. When we love someone who doesn't deserve it, serve someone who can never pay us back, or walk away from tempting sin, it matters. Even if we don't see a return for our efforts, the Lord is using it. One day, it will all come to light, and we can be sure of that.

Heavenly Father, what a glorious future you have in mind for all who place their trust in you! We know our toil is not fruitless; it has an eternal ripple effect. Thank you for the truth of your love, the guarantee of your promises, and the assurance of a life with you forever.

DISCIPLINE

Those whom I love I rebuke and discipline.
So be earnest and repent.
REVELATION 3:19 NIV

As humans, we are prone to pride. The majority of us are inspired by a desire for comfort more than anything else, and this is reflected in the concept of the American Dream. The radical life Jesus calls us to is not a life of comfort-seeking of but uncomfortable humility. He wants us to rejoice in his rebuke and to "be earnest and repent."

The more God loves us, the more he wants to perfect us. This perfection comes through trials or "rebuke and discipline." They are not easy, but they must be worthwhile if our loving God is willing to put us through them for his glory and our perfection. We should count it as a blessing to stand in the midst of discomfort and rebuke as this is evidence of the deepness of God's love for us. Imagine how radically different marriage could be if, instead of seeking comfort and satisfaction, a couple embraced difficulty together.

Dear Father God, please work in our hearts to change our outlook. Remind us that you rebuke those you love and teach us to appreciate this rebuke by being earnest and repentant.

A FUTURE HOPE

Certainly there is a future,
And your hope will not be cut off.
PROVERBS 23:18 NASB

Does believing that God has a future for you change the way you live? Does it impact the way you approach your marriage? Have you considered the future God has in mind for your spouse? How are you encouraging them toward their God-given future? Our trust in our heavenly Father is not poorly placed. We can have confidence and boldness as we walk toward our future in the Lord even if we do not yet understand it all.

In the same manner, we should strive to encourage, equip, and enable our spouses to walk forward into their destined future. Let us not become so narrow-minded that we misunderstand what God has for us individually as well as together as couples.

Almighty God, we ask for an encouraging glimpse into the future you have for us. Thank you for putting us together and for giving us hope and a future. We trust you each and every day as we walk forward into your perfect plan.

THE LIVING SPIRIT

The fruit of the Spirit is love, joy, peace, patience, kindness, goodness, faithfulness, gentleness, self-control; against such things there is no law.

GALATIANS 5:22-23 NASB

No one knew the Scriptures like the Pharisees did. They dedicated their lives to it, living in it, and breathed it in, yet they were "whitewashed tombs" (Mt 23:27). Their spirits were rotting inside of them while the outward façade of righteousness remained.

Many Christians in today's world are no different. It's possible to get up every morning to do our devotions, pray in the evening, and live morally right, yet have no connection to the spirit of God. The Pharisees lacked the fruit of the Spirit, the virtues of faith and obedience which only come from the Spirit of God living inside of us. When our lives are undisturbed, we may have the illusion that our spiritual lives are healthy, but then something or someone comes along to disillusion us, and we are left dumbfounded by our spiritual disease. It is a shocking yet necessary revelation. A good spouse, often more aware of our outward signs of righteousness than we are, is a critical source of these revelations.

Great and gracious Jesus, help us not be whitewashed tombs like the Pharisees. Let our spiritual lives blossom and grow with the fruit of the Spirit. When we are not living fully in the Spirit, may we help each other see the right path.

PRINCE OF PEACE

*God showed how much he loved us by sending his one and only Son
into the world so that we might have eternal life through him.*

1 JOHN 4:9 NLT

Christmas is a holiday associated with peace. But why? If we look
around at the commercialism and worldly influences surrounding
us, Christmas seems to be a holiday of anxiety, overwork, greed,
and discontentment. Where's the peace?

Well, where's your allegiance? It's one thing to say we follow Christ
but another thing entirely to take those necessary steps. We can't
live like the world and claim to serve the Prince of Peace. This
Christmas, let's drown out the world's woes with the peaceful
praise of the one who loved us enough to enter our chaotic mess.
Let's celebrate him for the eternal life and love he came to give us.

Dearest Savior, Prince of Peace, thank you for coming
to this world and offering us a way back to you. Thank
you for the permeating peace you fill us with which
the world can't understand. Please help us not become
distracted today with the world's version of Christmas.
We want to celebrate you!

LOVE IS A GIFT

Many waters cannot quench love,
nor can rivers drown it.
If a man tried to buy love with all his wealth,
his offer would be utterly scorned.

SONG OF SOLOMON 8:7 NLT

A lot of things can be said about love and what it means, but the most profound are examples of just how far someone is willing to go in the name of love. While human love has its limits, people are willing to put everything on the line for love.

The greatest example of love is Christ giving up his life for us. Solomon offers this beautiful, powerful description of love and its endurance. That should be what we aspire to in our relationship with God and with our spouses. We can't buy love, and in the case of Christ, we can't earn love either. Love is given as a gift.

Thank you for your undeserved gift of love, Lord Jesus. Thank you for the power of your love and your unyielding protection and provision for us. We do not deserve the love you give so freely, but we humbly and gratefully accept it.

FIGHTING FEAR

I sought the Lord and He answered me,
And rescued me from all my fears.

PSALM 34:4 NASB

Fear tends to steal our joy and overwhelm us with anxiety and uncertainty. Instead of trying to push through or deny our fear, let's bring it to God. After all, that is where our confidence and certainty come from. God fills us with courage and hope and outshines all the enemy's threats.

When we refocus our minds on Christ and his kingdom, the world and its woes grow dimmer. Nothing can stand against God, and God stands with us. It's not about ignoring our fear or trying to overcome it on our own; it's about directing our thoughts toward God instead of our fear and asking for his help.

We ask for your help today, Father. Fear is a monster that wants to consume us, but we are your children, and nothing can stand against your love.

GIVING

"In all things I have shown you that by working hard in this way we must help the weak and remember the words of the Lord Jesus, how he himself said, 'It is more blessed to give than to receive.'"

ACTS 20:35 ESV

Some responses come naturally while others take some work. Most of us like when things go our way: when we win the contest, get the promotion, or receive the gift. Even more excellent than coming out on top is giving to others. When was the last time you asked God for your spouse's success? Isn't it a great feeling when you give them a gift that truly blesses them? It means getting our minds off ourselves and putting in real thought and effort, but it's worth it.

Moving outward, how can the two of you be a blessing to other members of your family or community? What can you give? It takes work to choose to put the interests of others above our own, but that's what Christ was willing to do for the church, and we are not greater than he.

Teach us to concern ourselves with each other, Father, and to give more to our marriage than we expect to receive. May we find joy in giving of ourselves because of our love for you and for each other.

ONE BODY

Husbands also ought to love their own wives as their own bodies. He who loves his own wife loves himself; for no one ever hated his own flesh, but nourishes and cherishes it, just as Christ also does the church, because we are parts of His body.

EPHESIANS 5:28-30 NASB

Just as Christ loves the church, husbands should love their wives. In saying this, Paul sets the ultimate standard by comparing human marriage with how Christ treats us, the church. We all take time to care for our bodies by eating, washing, sleeping, and so on. Some people spend more and some less, but we all spend time, energy, money, and thought on taking care of ourselves.

To love another person as if they were one body with you, which is what marriage entails, means to have this same intentionality for them. True love is more than fuzzy feelings; it's sacrifice and submission. When we give our time, energy, and desires to someone else, we are on the cusp of understanding the love Christ shows us as his bride.

As husband and wife, God, we ask you to teach us to love each other more deeply. Teach us to care about each other's needs as if we were of the same body. We want to fully surrender to you by submitting to each other. That is how you demonstrated your love to us.

A Little Wrath

"With a little wrath I hid My face from you for a moment;
But with everlasting kindness I will have mercy on you,"
Says the LORD, your Redeemer.

ISAIAH 54:8 NKJV

The greatness of an offense determines the greatness of the punishment and resentment. In our case, we have all sinned against an all-powerful and perfect God. We have committed more egregious sins than we could count. God is perfect and infinite in his love for us, so his wrath is equally infinite. When God says "with a little wrath" in this passage, he is not bluffing. The measure of suffering the Israelites felt was a teaspoon of God's wrath meant to turn them back to their redeemer. He hid his face from them for a moment so the moment would lead to everlasting kindness and mercy. He would not be holy if he were not wrathful.

The same dynamic has to exist in our marriages. We cannot stand for any level of sin in our spouses, but we also have to shower them with kindness, mercy, and patience. If we want to dump the full measure of our wrath on them, we should instead remember God's course of action concerning us.

Lord, please make us this day into people of forgiveness who appreciate the wiping away of our sins for the miracle that it is. Thank you, God.

Purpose of Faith

*You love him even though you have never seen him. Though you
do not see him now, you trust him; and you rejoice with a glorious,
inexpressible joy. The reward for trusting him will be
the salvation of your souls.*

1 Peter 1:8-9 nlt

Can you say you have experienced a love that was unconditional, a love that knew no bounds, and joy and happiness that filled your heart to the absolute brim? Not everyone can. In fact, many people don't even know this sort of love exists.

As Christians, we can wholeheartedly attest to the existence of this love because we have experienced it firsthand. God's love does not care who you are or where you are from; it is for everyone from everywhere. He wants all his children to experience pure joy and genuine happiness, so he has commissioned us to share his love with everyone. How can you show your spouse unconditional love? How can you and your spouse together share God's love with the world?

Dear Lord, we are thankful for the gifts of love, life, peace, joy, and fellowship. Thank you for our marriage, our family, and our community. Thank you for enabling us to interact with you freely through prayer, showing us how to love our neighbors, and for this year of growing in our relationship with you. We look forward to another year with you and with each other.